Hot Seat:

The Practical Guide to a Homeowner Association Annual Meeting

Chris D. Gilleland

4523 Park Road, Suite 201A

Charlotte, NC 28209

704-347-8900

cgilleland@wmdouglas.com

Hot Seat: The Practical Guide to a Homeowner Association Annual Meeting

by Chris D. Gilleland

Professional & Tradesman Publishing & Media Company

Also, By Chris D. Gilleland

In the Arena: The Board of Directors' Guide to the Successful

Operation of a Homeowners Association

This book is dedicated to my parents, John & Rebecca Gilleland, and my son, Remington P. Gilleland.

No son could be more grateful of his parents than I am of my parents and no father could be prouder of a son than I am of my son.

Major-General Carl von Clausewitz

"Principles and rules are intended to provide a thinking man with a frame of reference."

Foreword

How is running a successful homeowner association annual meeting like baking a cake? Because in successfully baking a cake many small ingredients must be added, as with an annual meeting there are many different aspects that can be implemented that can achieve success.

While the analogy of baking a cake may seem oversimplified, it is not; tasks are simple, people make tasks complicated.

The author has been in this industry for over twenty years and has attended and chaired hundreds of annual meetings. One important aspect he has learned is that there is no magic bullet; there are many ingredients.

This book is structured in such a way it can be read outright page by page or read in sections on the particular topic of interest. This book is a practical reference guide on the homeowner association annual meeting process, with strategies and tactics to aid a board member or association manager in the successful operation of an annual meeting.

Acknowledgments

The author wishes to thank all those who contributed, especially my William Douglas Management team members, that inspired many of the best practices noted in this book.

The author wishes to thank Lydia Myrick and Ellen Linton for the line editing of this book. The author also wishes to thank parliamentarian Liz Guthridge of Connect Consulting Group, for her guidance on parliamentary procedure.

Contents

Disclaimer

This book is presented solely for educational and entertainment purposes. The author and publisher are not offering it as legal, accounting, engineering, insurance, construction or professional services advice. While best efforts have been used in preparing this book, the author and publisher make no representations or warranties of any kind and assume no liabilities of any kind with respect to the accuracy or completeness of the contents and specifically disclaim any implied warranties of merchantability or fitness of use for a particular purpose. Neither the author nor the publisher shall be held liable or responsible to any person or entity with respect to any loss or incidental or consequential damages caused, or alleged to have been caused, directly or indirectly, by the information or programs contained herein. No warranty may be created or extended by sales representatives or written sales materials. State statutes regarding homeowner associations can vary from one state to another so state statutes will need to be reviewed and may conflict with the material in this book. Every homeowner association is different, and the advice and strategies contained herein may not be suitable for your situation. You should always seek the services of a competent professional.

Attention

While this book is an overview of the homeowner association annual meeting process, it is no substitute for your particular state's statutes, if any, or any specific requirements of your association's governing documents. At numerous points in this book, the author recommends seeking guidance from the homeowner association's attorney. For specifics or clarification on any topic in this book, the guidance of an attorney experienced with homeowner association laws and procedures should be sought out.

By the very nature of the many thousands of writers of homeowner association governing documents and the potential of 50 different state statutes, unfortunately, some points in this book may conflict or be countermanded by a requirement of your particular homeowner association's governing documents or your state statutes. Again, for specifics or clarification on any topic in this book, the guidance of an attorney experienced with homeowner association laws and procedures should be sought out.

Intermingled Topics

Being a reference book, due to certain intermingled topics and for formatting continuity, certain topics could be cited more than once within this book.

Word Use

Use of "Generally, Usually," or "Typically"

Because of the many different state statutes governing homeowner associations and the fact that some states have no relevant statutes, the author is required to generalize on many points and topics. In addition, because of the many different attorneys producing association governing documents that almost guarantee that no two sets are written the same, the author is again required to generalize. Consulting individual state statutes or seeking guidance from an experienced association attorney for clarification may be needed.

Use of "Association"

For simplicity's sake, the term "Association" is used for all common-interest communities, such as single-family home associations, townhome associations, condominium associations, and co-ops.

Use of "Governing Documents"

Because declarations, bylaws and articles of incorporation have many different authors, and because particular provisions may be found in multiple documents, for simplicity's sake, in many places throughout this book the term "governing document" is used as a catch-all.

Use of "Board of Directors" and "Board"

Unless expressly noted, the use of board or board of directors refers to the executive board that governs a homeowner association. The terms "board" or "board of directors" are used interchangeably throughout this book.

Use of "Chair" and "Meeting Chair"

Chair and Meeting Chair refer to the Chairperson for an annual meeting unless expressly noted. The meeting Chair presides over the meeting and ensures that the rules of the homeowner association are being followed. The term Chair, Meeting Chair, Chairperson, Chairman, Chairwoman are all used interchangeably throughout this book. Chair is capitalized to emphasize the position throughout this book.

Use of "Meeting" and "Assembly"

Meeting and assembly are used interchangeably throughout this book.

Use of "CC&Rs" and "Covenants"

CC&Rs, Covenants, Covenants Conditions and Restrictions, and Declarations are used interchangeably throughout this book.

Use of "Assessment" and "Dues"

Assessment and dues refer to the membership's financial contribution to the operation of the association. These terms are used interchangeably throughout this book.

Chapters

CHAPTER ONE:
ANNUAL MEETING BASICS

Why is Properly Conducting an Annual Meeting So Important?

Many view the annual meeting with varying viewpoints and perspectives. One overwhelming aspect, often not contemplated or possibly realized, is the legal nature and the legal requirements of the annual meeting. First and foremost, an annual meeting is a legal proceeding, and if not properly conducted could possibly delegitimize the actions of the board of directors. For example, if the annual meeting was not properly noticed to the membership, and at this meeting, someone is elected to the board, are the future actions of this "elected" board member valid?

Parliamentary Procedure

Homeowner association annual meetings are to be governed by parliamentary procedure. Parliamentary procedure is the body of rules, ethics, and customs that govern most all deliberative assemblies. It can also be referred to as parliamentary law, parliamentary practice, legislative procedure or rules of order.

As in democratic societies, parliamentary procedure mirrors the same democratic principles, being that the majority rules with respect to the minority. This procedure allows for members of the assembly to maintain their rights while following the direction of the majority. Homeowner associations follow parliamentary procedure to debate and reach a membership consensus, usually by a vote. Simply put, membership voting determines the will of the assembly.

The rules of order within a homeowner association consist of rules typically drafted for the body by the association developer's attorney. These rules of order are most often referred to as the bylaws of the association. There could also be common rules of order issues addressed in other association governing documents, such as the CC&Rs. No two sets of homeowner association bylaws or rules are written the same.

An association's rules or bylaws go into detail about the operation of the homeowner association. A rule of thumb about association governing documents is that the CC&Rs tell who is responsible, while the bylaws tell how the association is to be operated or more precisely governed. It is common, and state statute may even mandate, that homeowner associations adopt a standard book or manual about parliamentary procedure, such as *Robert's Rules of Order*. These adopted manuals are consulted and adhered to when the homeowner association's governing documents, such as bylaws, are silent on a topic.

Robert's Rules of Order ("Robert's Rules") is reportedly the most commonly used procedural authority in use in the United States. This is, by far, the most common manual in use by homeowner associations.

Annual Meeting Fundamentals

- Because of the legal nature of an annual meeting, a businesslike atmosphere must be maintained at all times.

- The meeting Chair opens, directs and adjourns the meeting. To enable the Chair to direct the meeting efficiently, meeting procedures should be established at the beginning of the meeting. Homeowner association meeting procedures are typically grounded in *Robert's Rules of Order*. *Robert's Rules of Order* provides a systematic and efficient method of conducting a meeting. Meeting procedures ensure that important issues are addressed and use everyone's time effectively and efficiently.

- Only association business is to be brought up and discussed during the meeting. Items of an individual or personal nature that have no bearing on the entire association should not be discussed.

- The Chair prepares an agenda in accordance with the association's governing documents. The agenda outlines what is to be discussed. Without a written and focused agenda, the meeting can quickly go off-course.

- The Chair should point out to the membership at the beginning of the meeting that there will be an open floor discussion session at the end of the meeting which allows the membership to voice issues of a nature that involve and relate to the entire membership. The Chair should instruct the membership to hold questions until the open discussion. Allowing a member of the assembly to have the floor (allowing someone to speak) can be calamitous for the meeting. This is especially the case with contentious meetings.

Issues to Avoid:

- Legal matters. These issues are, by their nature, very sensitive. An annual meeting is NOT the forum in which to discuss legal matters involving association members or other parties. In the event a legal matter must be addressed, the association's attorney should be consulted and sign off on what is discussed. Having the attorney draft a statement to distribute is a good way to address a legal matter.

- Assessment delinquency of specific association members. State statutes address collection matters, and how this information is to be disseminated and the annual meeting format would typically not be acceptable.

Key Point: The role of the Chair is to maintain order by respecting and following the agenda. The Chair must overcome the concern of appearing rude or overbearing by calling people down who deviate from the agenda or speak out of order. The Chair must always recognize that any member who deviates from the agenda or speaks out of order is the one being rude and inconsiderate of the rest of the membership.

CHAPTER TWO:
THE GOVERNING DOCUMENTS

Homeowner Association Governing Documents

No two sets of association governing documents are the same. This non-uniformity is due to numerous factors. Primarily because of the many different attorneys drafting governing documents and the differences between each association. Moreover, the ever-changing nature of state, and possibly federal statutes, make uniformity of content impossible with governing documents.

Statute changes can alter or effectively make a provision of an association's governing document invalid. This is especially important considering that homeowner associations are a popular target of legislation. For example, in Arizona, the state legislator eliminated the use of proxies for annual meetings. This elimination of proxies was replaced by the implementing of absentee ballots.

Association Governing Document – The Basis of All Homeowner Associations

Covenants, Conditions & Restrictions (CC&Rs)

These are also known as CC&Rs, master deeds or declarations of covenants and other similar type names. By whatever name or abbreviation, these are written rules, limitations and restrictions on use, mutually agreed to (by virtue of purchasing in a homeowner association) by all owners of homes in the association.

CC&Rs may prescribe exterior home colors, pets, ages of residents, parking and other conduct in order to protect the quiet enjoyment of all the various members of the association. CC&Rs are generally enforced by the homeowner's association and, in extreme cases, by individual members who bring legal action against other association members or boards of directors. CC&Rs "run with the land" and thus are permanent for all practical purposes, so that future owners are held to the same restrictions. CC&Rs are filed with the register of deeds in the county in which the association is located.

Articles of Incorporation

This is the fundamental charter of any corporation (in the case of a homeowner association, a nonprofit corporation), which spells out the name, primary purpose, and incorporators. Articles must be signed by the incorporating person or persons or by the first board of directors. The starting point for filing and approval of articles of incorporation is usually the secretary of state in which the association is incorporated. However, not all homeowner associations are incorporated.

Bylaws

These are the written rules of conduct for a corporation. In other words, how the corporation is to be governed. They should not be confused with the articles of incorporation, which usually state the basic outline of the organization. Bylaws generally provide for meetings, elections of boards of directors and officers, filling vacancies, notices, types, and duties of officers, committees, assessments and other routine conduct. Bylaws are, in effect, a contract among members and must be formally adopted or amended. Bylaws may or may not be required to be on file with a government entity.

Rules & Regulations

The board of directors generally has the authority to establish reasonable rules and regulations. This authority is typically found in the CC&Rs. These rules and regulations may provide for the imposition of fines or penalties for the violation of the CC&Rs. While noted here for context, they do not play a role in annual meetings.

Governing Documents - Where to Start

The association's bylaws are typically, but not always, the governing document to be reviewed for the association's annual meeting requirements. The bylaws generally specify notification requirements, quorum percentage, and other specific meeting requirements.

The following is typical of what would be found in a homeowner association's governing documents. Key parts underlined for emphasis.

Section 5.0

Place of Meetings: All meetings of the membership shall be held at a place in Wake County, North Carolina designated by the Executive Board.

Section 5.1

Annual Meetings: A meeting of the Association shall be held at least once each year. The first Annual Meeting of the Association shall be held on the date and hour designated by the Declarant. Thereafter, the Annual Meeting of the Association <u>shall be held on the second Monday in February of</u> each year at 7:00 P.M. If the second Monday in February shall be a legal holiday, the Annual Meeting shall be held at the same hour on the first day following, which is not a legal holiday. At such meetings, the Executive Board shall be elected in accordance with these Bylaws, and the Members shall transact such other business as may properly come before them.

Section 5.2

Substitute Annual Meetings: If an Annual Meeting shall not be held on the day designated by these Bylaws, a Substitute Annual Meeting may be called in accordance with the provisions of Sections 5.3 and 5.4. A meeting so called shall be designated and treated for all purposes as the Annual Meeting.

Section 5.3

<u>Notices of Meetings: Written or printed notice stating the time and place of a membership meeting, including Annual Meetings, and the items on the agenda</u>, including the general nature of any proposed amendment to the Declaration or the Bylaws, any budget changes and any proposal to remove a director or officer, <u>shall be delivered</u>

not less than ten (10) nor more than fifty (50) days before the date
of any such membership meeting, either personally or by mail, by or
at the discretion of the President or the Secretary, to the address of
each Lot Owner. If not performed personally, notice shall be deemed
given upon deposit in the mail depository of each Lot Owner.

Notice given to any one tenant in common, tenant by entirety or oth-
er joint Owner of a Lot shall be deemed notice to all joint Owners of
the subject Lot.

The notice of meeting shall specifically state the purpose or purposes
for which the meeting is called.

Section 5.4

Quorum: Except as otherwise provided in these bylaws, the presence
in person or by proxy of Members entitled to cast twenty percent
(20%) of the votes, which may be cast for election of the Executive
Board, shall constitute a quorum at all meetings of the Members. If
a quorum is not present or represented at any meeting, the Members
entitled to vote, thereat, shall have the power to adjourn the meeting
from time to time, without notice other than the announcement at
the meeting, until a quorum is present or is represented. At sequen-
tial meetings following this failure to obtain quorum, the quorum
percentage is reduced by fifty percent. The Members at any meeting
at which a quorum is present may continue to do business until ad-
journment, notwithstanding the withdrawal of enough Members to
leave less than a quorum.

Section 5.6

Proxies: Members may vote either in person or by agents duly authorized by written proxy executed by the subject Member or by his duly authorized attorney-in-fact. A proxy is not valid after the earlier of the term stated therein or the expiration of twelve (12) months from the date of its execution. Unless a proxy otherwise provides, any proxy holder may appoint, in writing, a substitute to act in his place. To be effective, all proxies must be filed with the Secretary or duly acting Secretary, either during or prior to the meeting in question. A member may not revoke a proxy given pursuant to this Section 5.6, except by written notice of revocation delivered to the person presiding over a meeting of the Association.

All the above provisions concerning voting by joint Owners shall apply to the vote cast for any one Lot by two or more proxy holders.

Section 5.7

Majority Vote: The casting of a majority of the votes represented at a meeting at which a quorum is present, in person or by proxy, shall be binding for all purposes except where a different percentage vote is stipulated by these Bylaws, the Declaration, the Articles of Incorporation of the Association or the North Carolina Planned Community Act.

The CC&Rs and possibly the articles of incorporation may have annual meeting related provisions and should be reviewed as well. In very rare instances the bylaws may not reference the association's annual meeting in detail. In this case, if the other governing documents fail to address the annual meeting, the state's statutes for nonprofit corporations may be the only source for this guidance.

Conflicts sometimes arise if annual meeting language is found in multiple governing documents. For example, the bylaws may state the annual meeting quorum requirement is 10%, while the CC&Rs may state 20%. If conflicts arise, usually the declarations or the articles of incorporation take precedence over bylaws. When conflicts occur, it is best to seek legal counsel for specific guidance.

In certain situations, or for specific information, state statutes may need to be reviewed. For example, something as specific as to how long a proxy is valid. A state's statutes dealing with nonprofit corporations or state statutes specifically addressing homeowner associations would need to be reviewed.

CHAPTER THREE:
ANNUAL MEETING PAPERWORK & PROCESS

Annual Meeting Paperwork

This chapter deals with the typical paperwork and related process involved with annual meetings. Again, this is in general terms and each association's governing documents, or state statutes would need to be consulted to confirm any specifics. For example, California's Davis-Stirling statutes dealing with common interest developments may have additional mailing requirements that are unique just to that state.

While an annual meeting notice is usually required to be mailed, other items may be required to accompany this notice. Association governing documents, and possibly state statutes, could require additional items to be included. Even if there are no requirements, it is a good practice to include certain items, such as a nominating application and a proxy form.

Preliminary Steps Check Off Sheet

Association Name: _____

_____

Annual Meeting Preliminary Steps

Annual Meeting Date: _____ / _____ / _____

Annual Meeting Start Time: _____

Annual Meeting Location & Address: _____

_____

Location Closing Time or Time Meeting Must Be Over: _____

_____

Location Reservation Contact: _____

Location Reservation Contact Phone #: _____

Location Fee: $_____

Location Fee Check Cut Date: _____

Written Notification Time Requirements

No More Than _____ days before annual meeting

No Less Than _____ days before annual meeting

Notification Mailing Date: _____ / _____ / _____

Notification Mailing Items:

Notice of Annual Meeting _____

Nominating Application _____

Proxy _____

Double check association documents to make sure no other items are required to be mailed out with annual meeting notification mailing. For example: HOA Annual Budget, Agenda, etc.

Date Notification Items Mailed:

_____ / _____ / _____

Affidavit of Mailing Completed

Membership Communications

The importance of adhering to the association's governing documents and state statutes regarding notification requirements cannot be stressed enough. Not following the proper procedures and legal requirements can, at worst, have severe legal consequences, and at a minimum, cost the association additional expenses in correcting the matter. For example, having to call another meeting.

All association notices in a broad legal sense are used to communicate rights and responsibilities to an interested party. There are different forms of legal notice, with written notice being what is generally required by most associations. The definition of the term "written notice" can vary from state to state and even within different statutes of law within a state.

Official or required membership notifications are typically specified in an association's governing documents or the state statutes. For association operational issues, such as membership meetings, this information is generally found in the association's bylaws. If notification requirements are not specified in the governing documents, state statutes would be relied on for notification requirements.

Generally, the association bylaws are going to specifically outline membership notification requirements for annual meetings. Language similar to that below is typically what would be found in an association's bylaws. Key aspects are underlined for emphasis.

Section 3.2

Notices of Meetings: Written or printed notice stating the time and place of a membership meeting, including Annual Meetings, and the items on the agenda, including the general nature of any proposed amendment to the Declaration or these Bylaws, any budget changes, and any proposal to remove a director or officer, shall be delivered not less than ten (10) nor more than fifty (50) days before the date of any such membership meeting, either personally or by mail, by or at the discretion of the President or the Secretary, to the address of each Unit. If not performed personally, notice shall be deemed given upon deposit of a First-Class postage paid envelope in a United States Postal Service mail depository.

Notice given to any one tenant in common, tenant by entirety or other joint Owner of a Unit shall be deemed notice to all joint Owners of the subject Unit.

Effective Notice

Effective Notice or Effective Delivery is the term used to define that another party has properly been notified. The association generally has no responsibility to guarantee delivery or heed of a notice; only to make reasonable and prescribed attempts of notice as required in the governing documents. As specifically noted above in the sample bylaw language, notice shall be deemed given upon deposit of a First-Class postage paid envelope in a United States Postal Service mail depository. Even if the effective notice language in an association's governing documents is not specific to when placed in the mail depository, this is generally the accepted standard. The exception to this accepted standard is if governing documents have another specific procedure for notification. Anything less than a notice per First Class postage paid envelope mailed US Mail may not be sufficient for proper notice.

If the association's governing documents state: ...shall be delivered not less than ten (10) days..., per effective notice the ten days begin once the notices are placed in the US Mail, and not when the notice is received by the member.

Non-US Mail Notifications

With the advent of new technology, a common question is why annual meeting notices must be delivered US Mail if that is the only method per the association's governing documents. Especially considering all the communication technology such as email, text, instant messaging and association websites that essentially have no expense related to their utilization. Unfortunately, these methods of communication will, in most cases, may not meet the legal requirements of effective notice.

There are exceptions in which governing documents may prescribe alternative notice methods. These alternatives can range from posting signs at the entrances to the community, posting a notice on a community bulletin board or physically posting every member's front door with a meeting notice.

Even if the governing documents allow alternative forms of notifications, it can create concerns regarding effective notification. Effective notification can arise because of absentee owners not living within the association to see posted signs, members on vacation or even as simple as a member not using their front door for entry into their home and not seeing the hand posted notice.

In recent years various states have adopted statutes that have redefined effective notice. These new statutes address email delivery, website posting, and other electronic forms of communication. No matter what a state's statutes provide for effective notice, the association's attorney needs to review any changes to an association's traditional delivery method.

Annual Meeting Notice Process

Notice generally must be sent or heeded to all owners of record as listed on the membership roll. Generally speaking, notice of the association annual meeting should be in writing and is usually subject to a maximum and minimum notice period that varies by each association's governing documents. For example, maximum and minimum notice periods can be stated as: *Annual Meeting Notices can be mailed no sooner than 60 days before nor less than 10 days before the annual meeting.*

How an annual meeting notice is to be worded, or items that must be included, could vary from governing document to governing document, and from state statute to state statute. Or possibly the association's governing documents could have a specific example of the notice that is to be used. At a minimum, the annual meeting notice should clearly state a date, time, location address and the words: "Annual Meeting Notice." The notice should be formatted in such a way that the mailing could not be mistaken for something other than an annual meeting notice.

The importance of ensuring that the required wording and required delivery times are met cannot be stressed enough. If any of these aspects are not met, these failures could call into question the legitimacy of the meeting and all future board actions. Ensuring the accuracy of the meeting notice is another vital aspect of the process. For example, the meeting is called for Wednesday, June 9th, and Wednesday is actually June 10th can call into question the legitimacy of the meeting for improper notice. While a simple error, it is still an error that can raise questions about proper notice.

An error in the annual meeting notice is probably the most prevalent reason for annual meetings to be challenged. If an error is discovered in the notice, the meeting should be rescheduled, and a corrected noticed mailed. Correcting and rescheduling prevents the association meeting from being challenged in the future when correcting the matter may be much more difficult.

Example of an Annual Meeting Notice

Happy Glen Homeowners Association, Inc

P.O. Box 37109 Charlotte, N.C. 28237-7109 • 704/347-8900

May 12, 2019

TO: All members of the Happy Glen Homeowners Association, Inc.

FROM: The Homeowners Association Board of Directors

RE: Notice of Annual Meeting

The annual meeting is to be held on Wednesday, June 9, 2019, at 7:00 PM at First Baptist Church, Room 1009 located at 44609 Providence Road, Charlotte, NC 28270. Membership sign-in will begin at 6:30 PM.

All matters affecting the Association may be brought before the meeting and acted upon at the meeting unless specific notice of the same is required in the Articles of Incorporation, the Declaration, the Association's Bylaws or otherwise under North Carolina law.

If you cannot attend the meeting, you are urged to appoint a proxy to vote or otherwise act on your behalf as permitted by N.C.G.S. §55A-7-24. Your proxy will be effective when received by the Secretary or another officer of the Association and shall be valid until revoked in writing. You may revoke your proxy by (1) either attending the meeting(s) and voting in person or (2) by delivering a statement in writing that the appointment of the proxy previously delivered is revoked or (3) by appointing a new proxy in writing. You may not appoint the "Board" as proxy. You must appoint an individual. If you are unable to attend, please complete the enclosed proxy and submit to William Douglas Management.

This notice is being given pursuant to the requirements of the Association's Bylaws and N.C.G.S. §55A-7-05 this 12th day of May 2019.

Mary Smith, Agent of Happy Glen Homeowners Association

If a large membership turnout is common or expected, it is a good practice to note a membership "Sign-In" start time on the meeting notice. For example, Membership sign-in will begin at 6:30 to facilitate the meeting starting at 7:00.

Possible Additional Annual Meeting Mailing Items

Nominating Application

A Nominating Application, as the name might imply, is a form to be submitted prior to the annual meeting to submit names of members who are interested in serving on the board of directors. This type form may or may not be required to be mailed along with an annual meeting notice. However, this is an effective method to encourage association members to run for the board of directors. This proactive solicitation for board members can many times quash the perception that the board is self-perpetuating.

Example of a Nominating Application

Happy Glen Homeowner Association, Inc

P.O. Box 37109 Charlotte, N.C. 28237-7109 • 704/347-8900

NOMINATING APPLICATION

I, _____ owner of _____ hereby submit my name for consideration for nomination for the Board of Directors for the Happy Glen Homeowner Association Board of Directors, the election of which is to be held at the Annual Meeting on Wednesday, June 9, 2019.

Signed: _____

Address: _____

Date: _____

OR

I would like to nominate _____ of
_____ for consideration for nomination
to the Board of Directors for the Happy Glen Homeowner Association
Board of Directors, the election of which is to be held at the Annual Meeting on Wednesday, June 9, 2019.

I have previously discussed with him/her my intention to nominate him/her, and he/she has agreed to serve on the Board if elected and fulfill the duties thereof.

Signed: _____

Address: _____

Date:_____

Proxies

Proxies play an essential part in many association membership meetings. This is especially the case when associations have high quorum requirements and low membership meeting turnout. Because association governing documents vary, and individual state statutes vary as well, the following information is a general outline of the use of proxies within associations.

A proxy is the formal authority given to another party by an association member to act on their behalf in their absence at an association membership meeting. This party usually would not be required to be a member of the association.

While there is no universal or standard proxy form, in most instances this authority must be given in writing. The exception, unless prohibited by the association's governing documents, is in certain instances telephonic (by telephone) transmissions are permissible.

The proxy form must be signed by the member, either personally or by the member's attorney-in-fact. Generally speaking, a proxy form in electronic format that bears the member's electronic signature is considered valid in certain states.

A proxy is generally effective when accepted and filed by the association's secretary. Proxies can be written to be valid for a particular meeting or a longer time period. This time period can vary according to the association's governing documents or state statute.

A proxy is usually revocable by the member who appointed the proxy. Some governing documents and state statutes allow for, and some prohibit the use of irrevocable proxies. A proxy is revocable by the appointing member attending the meeting and voting in person or by the member delivering a written statement to the board secretary revoking said appointment. A proxy form can also be revoked by the member submitting a subsequent proxy form, which would automatically revoke the prior proxy when accepted and filed by the secretary.

If not prohibited by the association's governing documents or state statute, there are two types of proxies. First is the general proxy. A general proxy allows the appointed party the authority to vote as they see fit regarding any business brought before the meeting. The second type of proxy is called a limited proxy. With a limited proxy, the member directs the appointed proxy holder on how to exercise the proxy.

Wording that comprises a proxy form can vary; however, a proxy form should have a phrase similar to the following: "I John Smith, appoint Jane Jones as my proxy." The proxy should include a place for the member to sign and date the proxy. While state statutes and governing documents may have additional requirements, this wording would generally be the minimum.

Two primary concerns often arise when it comes to the use of proxies: first, members who submit proxies and do not attend meetings are less informed, and the second concern being members obtaining vast numbers of proxies and unduly influencing board election outcomes and other decisions of the assembly.

States and some associations have implemented limits on the use of proxies in attempts to reduce these two concerns. On occasion associations have amended their bylaws, preventing a party from using or limiting the number that can be utilized at a meeting. The state of Arizona implemented legislation that severely restricted the use of proxies in favor of mail-in ballots.

However, with both concerns taken into consideration, nonetheless, when a member signs a proxy form, they are giving their authority to another party to make decisions on their behalf. Short of a new statute or document amendment, there is not much an association board of directors can do to relieve either of these two concerns.

Proxy Forms

A proxy form is a form that when completed, gives a party the authority to represent someone else. The governing documents may require this form to be mailed out with an annual meeting notice. Some states may prescribe how proxies can be used or cannot be utilized at all. This can be the case even if the governing documents prescribe their use.

Example of a General Proxy Form

Happy Glen Homeowner Association, Inc

P.O. Box 37109 Charlotte, N.C. 28237-7109 • 704/347-8900

PROXY

N.C.G.S. §55A-7-24

The undersigned, pursuant to the Bylaws of the Association and pursuant to North Carolina General Statute §55A-7-24, does hereby appoint John Smith or _____ (in lieu of John Smith, if filled in) to vote or otherwise act for the undersigned owner(s) at any meeting of the Membership of the Association, including, without limitation, the meeting to be held on June 9, 2019, and any postponements or adjournments thereof. In the event a name is not inserted on the line provided, it is understood that he/she will act and vote in my/our stead.

Unless this Proxy is sooner revoked, as provided for in N.C.G.S. §55A-7-24, this Proxy will expire eleven (11) months from the date below. All other proxies signed by the undersigned are revoked and voided.

This the _____ day of _____, 2019.

_____

Owner (Printed Name)

_____

Owner (Signature)

_____

Property Address:

_____.

Example of a Combined General and Limited Proxy Form

Happy Glen Homeowner Association, Inc

P.O. Box 37109 Charlotte, N.C. 28237-7109 • 704/347-8900

PROXY

N.C.G.S. §55A-7-24

The undersigned, owner(s) of unit address: _____
_____ and member of Happy Glen Homeowner
Association appoints John Smith or _____ (in
lieu of John Smith, if filled in) as my proxy holder to attend the meeting of the membership to be held June 9, 2019, at 7:00 PM, at the First
Baptist Church, Room 1009 located at 44609 Providence Road, Charlotte, NC 28270

The proxy holder named above has the authority to vote and act for me
to the same extent that I would if personally present, with power of sub-
stitution, except that my proxy holder's authority is limited as indicated
below:

GENERAL POWERS - (You may choose to grant general powers, limited
powers or both. Initial below "General Powers" if you wish for your proxy
holder to vote on other issues which might be presented at the meeting
and for which a limited proxy is not required).

_____ If initialed, I authorize and instruct my proxy to use his or
her best judgment on all other matters which properly come before the
meeting and for which a general power may be used.

LIMITED POWERS - I SPECIFICALLY AUTHORIZE AND INSTRUCT MY
PROXY HOLDER TO CAST MY VOTE IN REFERENCE TO THE FOLLOW-
ING MATTERS AS INDICATED BELOW:

1. Do you want to approve the CPA firm recommended by the board of directors to perform the annual audit of the association's financials?

_____ YES   _____ NO

2.   Do you want to provide for less than full funding of reserves than is required by the Happy Glen Homeowners Association declarations of covenants?

_____ YES   _____ NO

Date: _____

_____

Signature of Owner

THIS PROXY IS REVOCABLE BY THE OWNER AND IS VALID ONLY FOR THE MEETING FOR WHICH IT IS GIVEN AND ANY LAWFUL ADJOURN-MENT. IN NO EVENT IS THE PROXY VALID FOR MORE THAN NINETY (90) DAYS FROM THE DATE OF THE ORIGINAL MEETING FOR WHICH IT WAS ISSUED.

Key Points About Proxy Forms

- In Lieu Of, If Filled In - A common issue with members submitting proxies is they may not know of anyone to appoint as their proxy. This issue can be overcome by the insertion of "in lieu of (name), if filled in." (See the following example for clarification)

- Appointing "Board" as proxy - This comes up, especially when an association member may not know the names of the board members or anyone else attending the meeting. The problem with appointing the "Board" is that there are multiple board members and appointing the board is not specific enough. An exception could be that a specific board officer, such as the secretary, is appointed. If there is a board secretary in office, this will generally be acceptable but could be challenged.

- Time Frame - It is common that proxies have a time frame of effect or expiration date. This, many times, will be dictated by state statute.

- Revoking a Proxy - A proxy can usually be revoked by the member who authorized the proxy attending the meeting or by submitting a sequential proxy form appointing another party. Or by a written statement revoking the proxy.

- Who Is the Proxy - Commonly misunderstood is that the proxy is not the completed form, but the actual person granted the authority.

- General Proxy Form - General proxies give blanket authority to the holder. Essentially the holder can vote however they see fit on any matter that may be undertaken at a membership meeting.

- Limited Proxy Form - A limited proxy, often referred to as a directed proxy, will commonly list the issues to be decided and how the proxy holder is to vote.

Affidavit of Mailing

In the context of a homeowner association mailing, an affidavit of mailing is a written sworn statement of fact, voluntarily made by the person responsible for the mailing. This affidavit attests that all meeting noticing requirements have been met and all the members were mailed such notices. The affidavit is witnessed as to the authenticity of the person's signature by a notary public.

A copy of all the items mailed and the membership mailing list should be attached to the affidavit. By adding these items, they become a part of the affidavit. Upon completing the affidavit, this should be placed in the permanent records of the association.

Even if the association's governing documents do not require this affidavit to be completed, it is an excellent procedural practice. If the notification aspect of an annual meeting is ever questioned, this can provide evidence to help support the association's compliance.

Example of an Affidavit of Mailing

AFFIDAVIT OF MAILING

I, _____, of lawful age upon his oath deposes and says: that he mailed to all _____ _____ property owners of record as of _____ _____, a letter containing information regarding the Annual Meeting of said Association to be held on this application on _____

. A copy of the typical letter and names and addresses of all _____
_____ property owners of record are
attached and made a part of this Affidavit.

That said mailing was made on _____.

_____

Signature

STATE OF NORTH CAROLINA) _____)ss
COUNTY OF _____)

The above and foregoing Affidavit as subscribed before me on this
_____ day of _____, _____, A.D. personally by _____
_____.

_____
                    Notary Public

My Commission Expires: _____

Membership Roll

The membership roll should be used to confirm membership of the association at the annual meeting. This is a continually evolving document with the buying and selling of homes within most associations. While the membership role may not always be completely current, it is the foundation of the annual meeting.

How the membership roll is used to verify membership may vary according to the association's governing documents or could solely be based on prior annual meeting practices. Whatever verification method is used, it is imperative that the quorum is established properly and not subject to question after-the-fact. Considering the distribution of voting instruments or other voting processes, this membership verification method is paramount to the integrity of the election process.

The most basic verification is a sign-in sheet where members sign their name and address. The association secretary will then match this sign-in sheet to the actual membership roll for confirmation. This is by far the least efficient method and generally unworkable for large membership gatherings.

Some homeowner associations utilize the roll call method for verification. As the name implies, the board secretary will call out each member's name and record present or not present. This method can work for smaller assemblies but can be unwieldy for large groups.

No matter the membership size, a membership roll printed with spaces for member's signature beside their name and addresses is the best method. This provides an efficient method to verify membership and allows for a permanent record of the quorum. In the Annual Meeting Preparation & Registration Chapter of this book, we will go into more detail about the sign-in sheet and how to use this method as efficiently as possible.

Ideally, sign-in sheets should allow enough space between names for members to comfortably sign their names. The sign-in sheet should be sorted according to last name in alphabetical order, with the last names highlighted. Highlighting the last name will assist the member in finding their name and will expedite the sign-in process. In the event a member's name cannot be found, a membership roll in address order should also be brought to assist in looking up by address. This most often happens when a home sells, and the new member's information has not been updated.

Ballots

Paper ballots are probably the most common method of voting used for board elections during the annual meeting. The two primary objectives of voting by ballot are secrecy and the documentation of the voting. Secrecy, because some members might be hesitant to vote if their vote was not confidential. Documentation, to allow precise voting and the ability to recount votes if necessary.

The association governing documents, or possibly state statute, may require voting to be by written ballot. If the governing documents do not stipulate the use of written ballots, this can be achieved by a majority vote, or by the assuming general consent of the membership. General consent being no objections from the membership of the use of ballots.

While there is no standard format for ballots, two key points should be considered when preparing: ease of marking and ease of counting. While both these points may seem self-evident, this is not always the case. Ease of marking, being that it is easily discernible whom to vote for and when counted, easily discernible how the ballot was cast. If there are preprinted candidate names on the ballot, the font size and space between these names needs to generous. If there are lines to allow candidate names to be written in, the space between lines needs to be generous.

Ease of counting is that the inspectors of election can accurately and efficiently count the ballots. Some of this "ease in counting" will be addressed with the font size and spacing, but the physical size of the ballot plays a part in counting. A standard full sheet (8.5 by 11) of paper, or possibly a half sheet, work best for counting. The author attended an annual meeting once where the board sought to save paper by printing ten ballots on a single sheet of paper. Not only were the ballots difficult to read and mark, but they also had to be counted multiple times. The membership was most annoyed by this as well, from not being able to read the small print and the filling-in of candidate names on a small piece of paper.

Another point about marking ballots is how members designate their candidate choices. No matter the written or verbal instruction about either circling their choices or placing an "X" by their selections and so on; people will always devise another method to indicate their preference, such as underlining the candidate's name or by placing an asterisk or star by their selection. For this reason alone, there should be plenty of space dedicated to each candidate so that the selection can be readily discernable.

It is a good practice for the voting instructions to be printed on the ballot. Instructions should be clear and written at an elementary school level. For example, "You can vote for up to three (3) candidates." Complicated or unclear instructions can lead to someone contesting the election after-the-fact.

If there are any special instructions or aspects required for voting, this information being printed on the ballot could be required by state statute or the governing documents. This could be the case even if the information is written elsewhere or explained verbally during the meeting.

Some larger homeowner associations have gone to the expense of having ballots printed that can be machine read. There are companies that offer these printing services and provide tabulation machines that allow for fast electronic vote counting. There can be issues with floor nominations and write-in nominees with this process, but it has the potential for speeding up the process.

Percentage Ownership and Ballots

There is a section of this book on the specifics of percentage ownership; however, emphasis needs to be placed here on how ballots play an intricate part of that process. Counting equal or unweighted votes can sometimes be a challenge, and tallying percentage ownership ballots can be a considerable challenge. With a little planning, calculating ballots based on percentage ownership can be achieved accurately and efficiently.

The first place to start with this process is the membership sign-in sheet. The percentage ownership should be noted by each member's name. This is so that when the member signs in, the ownership percentage is easily discernible by the person distributing ballots.

There are multiple ways to do this, depending on the number of percentage ownership categories or the total number of ballots to count. With more than 4 or 5 percentage ownership categories, hand writing the percentage on every ballot may be the only efficient method to utilize. If there are less than five percentage categories, ballots preprinted with the percentage noted on each ballot is an efficient method. For larger communities with limited percentage ownership, an additional tip to preprinting the percentage on the ballots is printing the ballots on different colored paper. The different colored paper can significantly assist in the counting of votes, which is especially the case in large communities.

A Delinquency or Aging Report

A delinquency report, also known as an aging report, is a report that lists the outstanding balances of association members. This report is the primary tool used by boards to determine which members are not current with their dues. The report is straightforward for the most part, but how it is utilized at an annual meeting may not be so straightforward.

Delinquency reports for an annual meeting come into play most often when determining if a member is in "Good Standing." There is a section in this book that specifically addresses the topic of members in "Good Standing." In short, a delinquent member may not be considered in "Good Standing," and thus this report is used to help determine this status.

What makes this process far from straightforward is the delicate nature of collections. This is primarily due to the laws surrounding collections. There are federal, and possibly state statutes, that govern public dissemination of delinquent parties. While homeowner associations do not fall under the Federal Fair Debt Collection Practices Act, there are still, however, state statute considerations. Unwarranted public debt disclosure could expose the association to liability. It is important to consider that collection laws are written to typically protect people who do not pay their debts, not necessarily to protect parties owed money.

The best course of action to avoid issues with disclosing a delinquent member is to note on the association sign-in sheet: "See Board Member" or see "Association Manager." This notation should achieve the desired effect without causing a disclosure issue. At this point, the member needs to be advised of the delinquent amount and what the policy is for rectifying the matter. Some governing documents may require a member to be current for a specific time period before the annual meeting, such as ten days, so paying at the meeting might not be an option. The qualifications for voting, such as being in good standing, should be noted on the annual meeting notice. Individually notifying delinquent members of this requirement by a secondary mailing is also a common practice of some homeowner associations and may be required by statute.

Welcome to the Annual Meeting Form

The quickest way for an annual meeting to get out of control is to deviate from the agenda by taking membership questions from the floor. This might be because the speaker may feel that not answering the question would be rude.

Another consideration is members interrupting the meeting may not realize that by doing so, they are out of order or doing something improper. Boards and association managers commonly overlook this and do not take into consideration the lack of meeting experience some members may have.

Members interrupting a meeting is a pervasive issue, and why this is so detrimental to a meeting is because it can derail the flow of the meeting. One member's question that is out of order creates another and so on. The meeting Chair must keep order and stay on the agenda or risk the meeting devolving into disarray.

Members attempting to disrupt the meeting, or who have personal animus, can cause havoc by interrupting the meeting. There is a critical procedural issue with allowing members to have the floor. Granting someone the floor is allowing that person to speak and address the assembly. If a member is well versed in *Robert's Rules of Order*, they could potentially shut the meeting down or cause other actions that would be in order because they were given the floor.

The following form, "Welcome to the Association Annual Meeting," is a great tool to help inform the members of these basics. Ideally, this form works best stapled on top of the meeting handouts. Never assume members in attendance know how the annual meeting process works.

Welcome to the Association Annual Meeting

Welcome. The Board wishes to thank you for your interest in the homeowner's association and attending the Annual Meeting.

The governing documents of our association have established the rules for how the meeting is to be held. There is a set agenda as dictated in your association's governing documents. Because of this, please do not interrupt the meeting unless you are addressed by the Chair of the annual meeting.

Please note at the bottom of the agenda there is an open floor discussion session which allows the membership to voice issues of a nature that involve and relate to the entire membership. During this open floor discussion, please avoid discussing issues that solely affect individual matters, such as individual maintenance, others in the membership, etc. Matters of an individual nature can be addressed after the annual meeting, or you can request to be added to the agenda of the next Board of Director's meeting.

Sincerely,

The Association Board of Directors

CHAPTER FOUR:
ANNUAL MEETING PLANNING

"Give me six hours to chop down a tree and I will spend the first four sharpening the axe." Abraham Lincoln

Annual Meeting – Board Planning

Efficient planning is true stress management, and this is the case with annual meetings. The board, even if the association is under professional management, must take an active role in the planning. This begins with reviewing the governing documents.

The governing documents may require meeting points that may or may not have been followed in the past. An example would be if the documents require that the board of directors form a nominating committee. The nominating committee is charged with finding members to run for the board of directors. If the governing documents have this requirement, this requirement should be complied with, no matter if it was not done in the past.

The directors should discuss everyone's upcoming role during the meeting. It is beneficial for the president and treasurer to provide the rest of the board with an outline of their reports. This will help ensure that all the board members are on the same page. For potentially contentious meetings, role playing the entire meeting is a good practice to help anticipate and plan for any issues.

If the association is under professional management, the association manager should be consulted for input. The association manager may offer pointers to improve the meeting. Prior board members may be a good resource for annual meeting preparation, especially on issues that were addressed before any of the present board members served.

Scheduling & Planning the Annual Meeting

Usually, an association's governing documents specify a particular day or month for the association's annual meeting to be held. The yearly anniversary from developer to membership control is sometimes used as the recurring time frame for this meeting as well. If no specific timing guidance is provided in the governing documents, it is customary that it be held around the date of the prior annual meetings.

If there is not a set day in the governing documents, or there is a way to select the day of the week, certain days of the week work better regarding attendance in the author's experience. Tuesday and Thursday nights tend to have better attendance rates than the other weeknights. Monday and Wednesday nights can work as well, although, with Wednesday, this can conflict with church attendance which can reduce membership attendance. Weekends are generally the worst for attendance, except for resort or vacation areas that might be more conducive to members being in town.

For associations that have a clubhouse large enough to accommodate an annual meeting, selecting a meeting location is usually not a factor. If off-site locations must be sought, churches are one of the best places to consider. Often, the rental fees are lower, and the location can be convenient for the association membership. An added benefit is in the event of a contentious meeting, members have been known to control their emotions better in church surroundings.

Meeting location may simply be determined by two factors, conveniences and cost. However, there is another factor that may need to be considered, especially if the meeting could be contentious: the ability of the meeting Chair to remove members disrupting the assembly from the room. Public places, such as libraries or community centers, may not allow for someone to be removed. This is even in the event the police are called to remove someone. While the likelihood of this becoming necessary is low, it is worth noting.

Annual meetings at restaurants and bars should be avoided. These venues usually have far too many distractions for an orderly meeting to be held. The possible consumption of alcohol can have a negative influence.

Annual Meeting Checklist

Check Sheet - Annual Meeting

Annual Meeting Check Sheet: Items to take or note

Association Name: _____

    __**Owner List Alphabetical Order with Signature Line**

    (Highlight names in yellow to make sign-in faster)

    __**Owner List by Address to verify against Alphabetical List**

    __**Returned Nominating Applications**

    __**Returned Proxies**

    __**Quorum Requirement:** _____ **% of Membership**

__**Quorum Requirement:** _____ **Actual Number in Person or by Proxy**

__**Percentage Ownership Spreadsheet to Calculate Quorum &** __ **Votes (If Applicable)**

__**Agenda * (Staple & make a packet of all handouts) Put Welcome to The Annual Meeting Sheet on top of the Agenda**

__**Last Annual Meeting Minutes ***

__**Ballots * (Check Documents to see if everyone gets one vote or if it's by percentage ownership)**

__**Association's Documents, CC&Rs, Bylaws and Rules & Regs.**

    __**Last 12/31 Income Statement ****

    __**Current Budget ****

    __**Last Complete Month's Balance Sheet**

    __*Robert's Rules of Order*

___Notice of Annual Meeting with Affidavit of Mailing

___Recent Audit Report

___Blank Proxies and Blank Nominating Application ***

___Delinquency Owner List ****

___Double check association documents to make sure no other items are required to be provided to membership during Annual Meeting. For example, a copy of last year's audit.

* Number of Copies: Estimate of total attendance plus 20% more

** Number of Copies: Determined by what board wants to distribute

*** Five copies for members who come and must leave

**** If governing documents and board of directors require this for voting

Nominating Committee

A nominating committee is a committee that is formed under the authority of the association's governing documents. While some governing documents will not address a nominating committee, others will mandate the committee be established. The governing documents may provide for how the committee is to be formed. The governing documents may allow for the members of this committee to be appointed by the board of directors. However, a better practice is for the nominating committee to be elected by the membership. If elections are not feasible, seeking volunteers from the membership would be the next best alternative. This helps avoid any appearances of conflicts of interest. The committee is perceived as more objective by the act of encouraging membership involvement in the process. Even if the board of directors has the authority to appoint, any board member that will be a nominee in the upcoming election should abstain from voting. They should also not be involved with the committee beyond the level of what any other nominee would have.

A nominating committee is formed to evaluate and seek out candidates to run for the board of directors at the annual meeting. The duty of the committee is to seek out candidates who have the abilities and interpersonal skills to benefit the operation of the board of directors.

The board of directors should provide the committee with a membership list, description of duties and any other requirements. They should specify to the committee the requirements as established in the association's governing documents. Requirements could range from nominees being in good standing to nominees having residency requirements. There could be requirements that are difficult to ascertain, such as no criminal convictions. Whatever the requirements, a written summary should be presented to potential nominees to avoid any issues going forward that may disqualify them from serving on the board.

The committee or at least one committee member should meet with potential nominees and review the requirements to serve. The committee should also gauge their abilities to serve along with their desire to serve. The committee should secure a commitment to serve from the potential nominee before presenting the report or recommendations to the assembly. No member should be nominated without their consent to serve if elected.

At the annual meeting, the nominating committee may have a formal role or may provide their report to the meeting Chair. If there is a more formal role, typically the committee chair addresses the assembly at the appropriate point in the agenda. The committee chair, traditionally, will state the nominee's name and that the nominee has agreed to serve if elected. The annual meeting Chair or the inspectors of election should repeat the names to the assembly.

The membership will typically have the opportunity to nominate additional candidates from the floor to supplement the committees. The primary consideration is that if the governing documents require a nominating committee to be formed, the board of directors should form this committee. While the committee may not find any candidates, it must be established for that purpose.

Forming a nominating committee, even if the governing documents have no such requirement, is a good practice. A formal nominating committee can seek out and qualify candidates to ensure they can devote time, energy and other resources to the association. Entirely relying on floor nominations can result in uncertainty, while a nominating committee can seek out the best possible candidates.

Typical Candidate Questionnaire

Sample Candidate Questionnaire

1. Please print your name as you would like it to appear on the ballot:
_____

2. How long have you been an owner in Happy Glen HOA? _____
Address: _____

---

3. Please indicate other experience - board, committee, career or community that you feel will benefit the Association if elected:

4. How do you feel you can contribute to the Board of Directors?

5. Please list your goals for the Association if elected:

What to Distribute at an Association's Annual Meeting

What to distribute at an annual meeting can vary from association to association. Many times, this is due to prior practices of what was distributed at previous meetings, as well as what may be required per the association's governing documents or state statute.

The first place to check is the association's governing documents. The bylaws, the covenants and possibly the articles of incorporation may address this type of issue. The sections in these documents that address the annual meeting may go into great detail about what is to be distributed at the meeting.

Using the governing documents as the basis, the board can fine-tune what is to be distributed. This is possibly taking into consideration what was distributed at prior annual meetings. While considering what was distributed in the past may not be required per the governing documents, it may cause consternation among the membership if a popular prior practice is not continued.

While the requirements can vary, the following are generally the normal items to be distributed: The Agenda, current or upcoming year budget, year-end financial reports (typically a balance sheet and an income statement), approved minutes from the prior annual meeting and, of course, ballots for the board elections.

Take 20% more materials, agendas, and ballots than the attendance at the last annual meeting, unless a larger crowd is expected due to an unusual situation facing the association that would increase attendance.

Distributing Surveys at the Annual Meeting

Surveys accomplish two important things: first, to gauge the membership, and second, to give members ownership in the process. Assessing the membership on different aspects of their association experience can be a great barometer to membership sentiment, as well as a great learning tool. The second aspect of ownership in the process is probably one of the least appreciated elements; simply stated, people appreciate the opportunity to be heard. Even if what people espouse in a survey is not necessarily acted upon, the vast majority appreciate the opportunity to voice their opinion. This helps to build inclusiveness within the membership. It may also reduce concerns from members who do not feel they are being heard.

Another excellent point about distributing surveys at an annual meeting is that generally a more balanced response is received. Balance, being more representative of the entire membership. Many times, when they are distributed via email, US mail, Survey Monkey, and so on, the surveys tend to be returned by a disproportionate number of members who have an axe to grind. Percentage-wise, more members complete and return surveys at annual meetings than any other delivery method, many are completed while members are waiting for the meeting to start.

Ideally, surveys should be under ten questions and have as many predetermined answers that can be checked for ease of completion. Surveys with more than ten items, or with too many fill-in-the-blanks questions, are less likely to be completed. Using more 'form' questions also make compiling less cumbersome. See an example of a Membership Survey in the Appendix.

A Homeowner Concerns Form

An excellent tool for annual meetings is the Homeowner Concerns Form. There is an example of this form in the Appendix. This form has two practical purposes. First, it reduces members wishing to speak at open discussion about matters of an individual nature, such as a neighbor dispute. This form can be mentioned when the Chair at the beginning of open discussion announces that only issues affecting the entire association should be discussed. Thus, providing those members with individual issues an alternative to open discussion. Second, this form is a benefit to those members who are reluctant to speak in front of the membership for whatever reason.

Committee Sign-Up Sheet

An annual meeting is an excellent opportunity to get more of the membership involved with the community. First, there is a room full of members who showed enough interest in their community to attend the annual meeting. And second, it gives members who are unhappy with an aspect in the community to participate by signing up to serve on a committee.

If a member attends the annual meeting, they are more apt to want to participate on a committee, as opposed to other members who feel no need to attend. One underappreciated benefit of members serving on committees is that it is an excellent foundation for serving on the board of directors. By serving on a committee, it will be easy to gauge how the member works with others and contributes to the committee. Their service on the committee will typically reflect how they would serve on the board of directors.

When members are concerned, or possibly complaining, about an aspect of the association, their service on a committee should be sought out. Make these members a part of the solution. If nothing else, they are given the opportunity to participate, whether they choose to or not. The author has attended many meetings where a member is angry about some aspect of the association. However, when openly invited to serve on a committee to address their concerns, more often than not, the member refuses to serve. The author has seen the wind let out of many sails when the rest of the members realize that a member just wishes to complain without contributing to a solution.

If nothing else develops from putting out a sign-up sheet, at least it lets the membership know the board wants their help and input. Sign-up sheets do not need to be elaborate, only functional with just the basics such as name, address, phone number, and email. These sign-up sheets should be placed away from the membership sign-in area to avoid creating backlogs in that process. They are typically placed on the table with the annual meeting handouts.

In the author's experience, sign-ups have about a 20% follow through rate, meaning people who sign-up actually follow through with their commitment. While 20% may not seem like a significant and successful percentage, it is a great start. If one or two excellent volunteers develop from an annual meeting sign-up sheet, it is well worth the minimal effort.

Maintenance Request Sign-Up Sheet

Providing maintenance sign-up sheets can help address any maintenance needs by the membership. This will reduce members bringing this topic up during open discussion.

Open Discussion Sign-Up Sheet

This is discussed in more detail in the Open Discussion section of this book. The Open Discussion Sign-Up Sheet should have a place for the member's name, address, and topic they wish to discuss.

CHAPTER FIVE:
MEETING ROOM PREPARATION & REGISTRATION

Annual Pre-Meeting Operational Points

- Contact the meeting location at least 10 days before annual meeting date to verify reservation is in order along with any other pertinent details.

- Show up at least 45 minutes to an hour before meeting start time.

- Have copies and information (Handouts) gathered a day before the meeting. (Stress Management Tip)

- Staple handouts (i.e., Welcome to the Annual Meeting Form, Agenda, Minutes, Balance Sheet) together. This will move people through the sign-in line faster. This will also help move the meeting along because everything will be in order.

- Set up a table away from the sign-in table for handouts, surveys, work-order sign-up sheets, committee sign-up sheets, and open discussion sign-up sheets. Placing these items at the sign-in table can cause a backlog by members stopping to look through the material.

Room Setup – An Orderly Meeting

Seating may appear to be inconsequential but arranging the seating can be one of the more critical aspects of an orderly meeting. Not surprisingly, configuring the seating is one of the simplest elements, and also the least utilized, of an efficiently controlled meeting. The meeting space and seating configuration must support the meeting's purpose. The membership's comfort and ability to listen must be considered; however, configuring the room for maximum meeting control is most beneficial, especially if the meeting is possibly contentious. The right configuration can have the effect of calming upset members and keeping a rowdy crowd under control.

The first point of configuring any room is that the meeting Chair needs to be able to move freely around the room. Ideally, the Chair should not place anything between themselves and the membership, no podium or table to "wall themselves off" from the audience. Being able to move among the membership helps the Chair and the assembly connect in a positive way. Any barrier, or even an elevated platform, unnecessarily distances the Chair from the audience. In certain situations, and specifically with large room configurations, the use of podiums and platforms may be necessary.

The audience seating should be arranged with an aisle down the center. If there is a possibility of the meeting being contentious, the fewer seats in the back row the better. Essentially, eliminating a back row by arranging chairs in a semicircle is the most advantageous configuration. From the author's experience, instigators generally sit in the back row.

The most conducive configuration for an extremely contentious meeting is a seating circle. A seating circle is arranging the chairs in a circle, with the speakers standing in the center. The theory is that when everyone is essentially facing everyone else, he or she is more apt to put on their best face. Unfortunately, even with adding multiple rows to a seating circle, they are usually not practical because of the number of attendees and room-size limitations.

Examples of meeting room configurations can be found in the Appendix.

The author works with an association that holds their annual meeting in their municipality's meeting room. The space is exceptionally nice. The city council sits on a dais that the board of directors utilizes during their meeting. The dais is very elaborate with ornate wood panels that places a barrier between them and the audience. The dais is so high that a person of average height while standing, must look slightly up to make eye contact with the people sitting behind the dais. Typically, a dais this overpowering would be in a very large room; however, this room holds about thirty chairs. A common complaint from the membership is that they feel they are figuratively and literally being spoken down to from on high by the board of directors.

Registration Process/Membership Sign-In

Membership sign-in may seem like just another insignificant process and not a crucial aspect of the annual meeting, but nothing could be further from the truth. A well-executed registration can help set a positive tone for the entire annual meeting. This is one of the first impressions members receive when they arrive, and excessive waiting and disorder can cast a less than positive light on the proceedings.

This less than positive light can be magnified if the membership is riled up about some other association matter. Waiting in a long line to perform a mundane task, such as signing one's name, is never conducive to cheering people up. Think of the line at the DMV.

The ultimate objective is for a smooth and seamless process. It is possible for members to sign-in and be through this process in less than 15 seconds. There are a number of tactics for sign-ins that are effective and simple to implement.

No matter the number of members of the association, there are steps that, if followed, can improve the efficiency of the meeting. The sign-in sheet should be in alphabetical order by name, along with the member's home address. Only the names should be highlighted in yellow to help assist the member finding their name. Signature lines need to be wide enough apart to allow for quick signing.

Write in a bold color at the top of each sign-in page, the first three letters of the member's last name that is at the top of the page. Then note the first three letters of the member's last name that is at the bottom of the page. For example, "ADA through BAK." This little notation can save a great deal of time for members searching for their names.

If feasible, taping sign-in sheets to tables allows for expedited registrations. The tables should be labeled as "A-B" table, "C-D" table and so on. Multiple pens should be distributed on each table, so that essentially dozens of members are signing-in at the exact same time, leaving no need for a line.

The author works with a homeowner association that has around 2,500 members and holds their meetings in a school cafeteria. The lunchroom tables are moved into the hallway leading into the cafeteria. The sign-in sheets are taped to all these tables, which provides a great way to expedite this process. There is an A thru B table, C thru D table and so on. Sign-in begins at 6:30 and is typically completed by 7:00. The last annual meeting had over 700 members in attendance, and the meeting was called to order at 7:02.

If feasible, try not to have members in the registration line standing in the elements. Many times, merely moving the registration table further into the building will prevent this from happening. Members who become either hot, cold or wet while waiting to sign-in may not have the happiest disposition for the meeting itself.

Most association annual meetings have paper handouts with the related meeting material, such as an agenda, budget, and so on. These items should be moved as far away from the sign-in area as feasible. Members collecting these items can cause a bottleneck, with members reading and shuffling the papers. These handouts should also be stapled together to speed up this process.

If proxy forms are submitted beforehand, noting this on the sign-in sheet before the meeting improves the process drastically. This notation should be entered beside the member's name who is assigning their proxy. For example, John Smith is the proxy for Mary Jones, beside Mary Jones' name on the sign-in sheet write: "John Smith - Proxy." Once John Smith arrives at the registration, he should sign his name on Mary Jones' signature line, as he is accepting her appointment as proxy.

Besides bringing the sign-in sheet in member alphabetical order, a list of the membership by address should also be brought. Many times, this will catch names that are recorded incorrectly on the membership rolls, such as a misspelling or a jumbled name. Jumbled name, such as being listed as "Terry Martin," when it should have been listed as "Martin Terry." This street address list will also catch when the membership roll has not been updated with a new homeowner.

What can be done when people arrive at the annual meeting, and they are not on the membership roll? Having access to the Internet to check the county's register of deeds website sometimes does not help, due to a 'lag time' between a home sale and the site being updated. Issues could arise about the timing of when a home legally transfers ownership. In some states, a home is legally transferred at the delivery of the deed, or when the deed is recorded, and in some states, it may be lawfully transferred at closing.

Other issues arise around special types of home purchases, such as an installment contract to purchase. While the buyer in an installment contract may have equity in the home, typically the name on the title or deed is still the legal owner. The association's attorney may need to clarify ownership in these cases in certain states.

In the event a name is not on the membership role because of a possible error or unrecorded real estate transfer, the board can implement a rule for provisional ballots. Provisional ballots are the same as regular ballots except they are marked as such. "Provisional Ballot" should be written on the ballot along with the name and address of the person. Until their ownership can be verified, the membership roll cannot be updated, and their ballot needs to be set aside during the ballot counting. In the unlikely event that this provisional ballot is consequential, it can be decided before the election if this provisional ballot will need to be verified. The reasoning behind provisional ballots is to avoid potentially disenfranchising a member.

If the association's governing documents prevent members who are not "In Good Standing" from participating in the annual meeting, this matter needs to be addressed at sign-in and before a ballot is distributed. The most prevalent reason for this situation is that members are delinquent in paying their assessments. If this is the case, for obvious reasons, this should not be noted on the sign-in sheet. Beside the member's name, it should be noted: "See board member or association manager."

Generally, the fewer people distributing ballots the better. The people responsible for distributing ballots' primary focus must center around watching members sign-in and only distributing a ballot once someone does sign-in. This particular process is crucial to the integrity of the election.

If a member owns multiple homes, or a member has a substantial number of general proxies, it is usually acceptable to provide one marked ballot noting such. For example, the ballot could note in the top portion: "14 Votes." This wording needs to be initialed by the person who is distributing ballots, so it can be verified if the need arises.

In condominium associations, percentage ownership is a factor in most sign-ins and especially when distributing ballots. When preparing the sign-in sheet for a meeting, recording the member's percentage ownership beside their name will help speed this process. By doing so, all the person who is distributing ballots must do is look for the percentage ownership beside the name once the member has signed-in. Having this data prefilled in will aid in the calculation of quorum as well.

Another good practice is having preprinted ballots with the percentages already written at the top of the ballot. This can be done with individual ballots noting one percentage ownership at the top. It can also be done with ballots listing all the percentage ownerships with the ability to mark or circle the ballot recipient's percentage. The person distributing the ballots will be responsible for noting the corresponding percentage when handing out.

The sign-in is the first impression the membership has upon arrival, and if it is being handled smoothly, it can set a positive tone for the entire meeting. The flipside of this is while the members may not even realize when sign-in is being handled smoothly and efficiently, they do recognize when it is not.

> **If there is ever a question about someone being a member of the association or a party authorized to represent a member, the best practice is to provide that person with a marked provisional ballot noting name and address that can be withdrawn if the situation proves to warrant the withdrawing of the ballot.**

Quorum

A quorum is the number of members required to be present before a meeting can legally be conducted. Quorums are necessary for annual membership meetings to be held. If association business, such as a vote, is to be conducted, special membership meetings would require a quorum as well. There does not have to be a quorum of the board of directors for an annual or special membership meeting. They are in fact a membership meeting and only need a quorum of the membership.

Annual membership meeting quorums can be almost any percentage of the membership. Membership meeting quorum requirements can range from as little as 5% and up. It is not unheard of to have a 75% quorum requirement in some older governing documents. Quorums are typically going to range from 10% to 20%.

Special membership meetings may have a higher quorum requirement than an annual meeting. This is typical when special meetings are held to raise dues or vote on a special assessment. This higher quorum threshold is especially common if the annual meeting quorum requirement is exceptionally low.

The purpose or necessity of having a certain quorum percentage is to confer decisions made in a meeting the authority to be binding. Thus, if a quorum is not present, no association business can legally be conducted. If business is conducted, such as board elections, these elections can rightly be challenged as improper. Any decisions these "board members" make going forward could be illegitimate and could consequently delegitimize any decisions that a properly elected board member would make.

A proxy is authorization from an association member to another party, not necessarily another association member, to act or vote in their place. Unless the governing documents prohibit a proxy's use, proxies can be used for annual membership or special membership meetings to help establish a quorum.

If the meeting quorum is difficult to obtain because of a high percentage requirement, a common acceptable means to help meet quorum is the "member in good standing" provision found in many governing documents. This provision will often have wording similar to: "*A Member shall be considered to be a Member in Good Standing if such Member is not past due in their assessment or not in litigation with the association.*" If there is not a standalone in good standing provision, the section regarding membership voting rights will many times be worded similar to: "Only members in good standing are permitted to participate in the annual meeting." This can reduce a quorum requirement by reducing the number of homes that are factored into the quorum.

For example, in a 100-home association, the quorum requirement is 25%, which equates to 25 members in person or by proxy for a quorum. If 10 members of the association are not in good standing, this quorum is factored on 90 homes instead of 100, which reduces the required number from 25 members to 23 members to constitute a quorum. If the governing documents are not clear on which members can and cannot vote, the association's attorney should be consulted for clarification.

Another possible solution to high quorum requirements is if the annual meeting provision in an association's governing documents allows for subsequent annual meetings. This provision allows for follow-up annual meetings at a lower quorum requirement if a quorum is not obtained at the initial annual meeting. If there is such a provision, the quorum is many times halved or at least reduced on subsequent annual meeting attempts.

If there is no specific percentage quorum requirement addressed in an association's governing documents, and no state statute provides guidance, the quorum traditionally defaults to 51%. Some states have statutes regarding quorums of homeowner association meetings that could potentially lower the quorum threshold, no matter what is maintained in the governing documents.

When calculating quorum always round down.

So, 49.9999% is going to be 49%.

When There is No Quorum

Business cannot be conducted at an annual meeting when a quorum is not achieved. The quorum requirement could be a high percentage that is difficult to achieve, or there could be apathy in the membership, and thus, a low turnout. Whatever the reason, there may be methods that can be used to have a "meeting" or even obtain quorum.

Associations can be burdened with two situations that make achieving a quorum for the annual meeting difficult: a high quorum percentage or membership apathy that results in low attendance. It is not unheard of to have unrealistic annual meeting quorum requirements of 50% to 75%. Almost all associations are subject to a little membership apathy at one time or another.

When low membership turnout is a problem, many boards look to amend the governing documents as a solution. Unfortunately, if low membership turnout is the problem, many times it is difficult to amend, because a meeting with high turnout may be needed to pass an amendment. However, to amend to lower an exceptionally high quorum percentage, the amendment process is generally a worthwhile goal for the board to pursue.

If the quorum requirement is at an acceptable percentage and the association is just intermittently plagued by apathy, an amendment may not be the best course of action. Working on increasing membership attendance, as covered in another section of this book, may be a better strategy. If an association has a 10% or even a 20% quorum, not much is achieved, proportionally, by lowering. Better results could be achieved by an aggressive proxy campaign or another attendance boosting method.

No matter the circumstance of why a quorum is not achieved, there is a common "make do" remedy that can be called upon, a board meeting in lieu of the annual meeting. If a quorum of the board is present, the board of directors may decide that having another attempt at an annual meeting is either not practical for the reasons discussed, or possibly is not economically prudent. Economically prudent, in that the additional notice mailings, room rental, and labor expenses cannot be substantiated on the concern that the quorum result will be the same as the first meeting.

Board meeting in lieu is, of course, acceptable if the association's governing documents, or even state statute, do not address or specifically mandate follow-up annual meeting attempts, or if sequential meeting attempts do not have a reduced quorum provision. If the governing documents have language that significantly reduced quorum percentages, a quorum may become more obtainable.

Board meeting in lieu of an annual meeting is simply when an annual meeting does not obtain quorum; therefore, the board calls a board meeting and covers the topics of the annual meeting. The exception being the board elections or any other matter on the agenda that would require the consent or vote of the membership.

In practice, the meeting Chair would first call the annual meeting to order. The Chair would then verify that a quorum was not achieved and announce such to the those in attendance. The Chair would then adjourn the attempt at an annual meeting. At this point, the board can decide to call a board meeting in order to disseminate the information on the annual meeting's agenda. If the board decides to proceed with a board meeting instead of attempting another annual meeting, the Chair should be prepared to explain the rationale behind this decision to those in attendance. The Chair should clarify that the annual meeting agenda will be used, and the elections and any other association business on the agenda that requires membership action or consent will be removed.

The board may wish to solicit names of members wanting to serve on the board, and if there are any board vacancies, consider those names submitted and decide at a future board meeting to appoint. Appointments would have to be in accordance with the board's ability to appoint from the governing documents.

During this board meeting, boards have been known to hold the annual meeting elections as scheduled and allow the membership to vote. This "election" is done with the understanding that at the next scheduled board meeting the departing board members will resign and the remaining board members will appoint the members who were selected by the membership. The issue with this pseudo-election process is that it can result in the board losing creditability if the board does not follow through with the resignations and follow-up appointments. All too often a board member does not wish to resign, or the board does not want to appoint one of the winners of the pseudo-election.

Again, there must be a quorum of the board of directors to hold this board meeting in lieu of. Moreover, there are no governing documents or state statute requirements that would require further meeting attempts. For follow-up appointments of directors, the governing documents would need to allow for the board to appoint for board vacancies.

If any member of the assembly objects to the board meeting in lieu of process, the board could decide to attempt another annual meeting and still have their board meeting 'in lieu of' for that particular time and place. The reasoning being that even though the assembly did not obtain quorum, the board can still disseminate the information. This is especially practical considering the expense incurred to call the initial meeting into question. It is quite common that attendance typically decreases at every sequential meeting attempt, making quorum even more difficult to achieve. The exception being if members aggressively go out and solicit proxies.

Typical Reduced Quorum Language

Article 5.1 Quorum for the association annual meeting is 25% of the membership, in person or by proxy. If any meeting of the association cannot be organized because of a lack of a quorum, the owners who are present, either in person or by proxy, may adjourn the meeting, from time to time, until a quorum is present. The quorum for a meet-

ing, following a meeting adjourned for lack of a quorum, is half the requirement of the prior meeting.

Quorum Hocus-Pocus

There are notification and quorum provisions in governing documents written in such a way that some mistakenly believe they can be manipulated to achieve the desired result. Some of these "tricks" may even be espoused by professional management companies. One example is to adjourn the attempt at an annual meeting and immediately call another annual meeting into order. The most common document wording used to justify this is, "may adjourn the meeting from time to time until a quorum is present." The problem usually stems from the membership meeting notification period not being met.

In this same vein, the author has seen notices mailed with multiple meeting times noted in the event a quorum is not met. For example, first attempt 7:00, second attempt 7:01, third attempt 7:02 and so on. Most of these tricks are questionable practices at best. Even if a professional management company recommends a practice that does not appear to be in the spirit of the governing documents or the spirit of the law, the association's attorney should sign off on this as well. The association's attorney should be confident that the trick will stand up if challenged.

If the governing documents do not allow for quorum reduction, amending the documents may be the only viable option.

Absentee Ballots May Count Towards Quorum

Certain state statutes and governing documents may allow for absentee ballots to be counted towards quorum. If statutes and the association's documents do not specify absentee ballots can be used for quorum, ballots can many times be drafted to indicate as such. The association's attorney should be able to draft additional language on the ballot that can accomplish this task.

Who Can Attend?

Questions arise about who is permitted to attend annual meetings. This often occurs when boards wish to prevent certain non-members from attending. Tenants and other non-member residents, such as co-habitants, are usually the focus of this concern. Unless a non-member has a valid proxy form appointing them as a member's proxy, they generally can be denied admittance to the assembly. The Chair would enforce this rule. The association governing documents need to be reviewed for any possible provision that would allow non-members to attend.

CHAPTER SIX:
THE ANNUAL MEETING, AN OPERATIONAL OVERVIEW

Front Door Solutions

One of the most effective tactics that the board of directors and association manager can utilize is the impact of first impressions when members arrive. This may seem like a minor point; however, being at the door speaking with members upon arrival can go a long way in setting the tone for the entire meeting. The author has found it common at contentious meetings that the board is at the furthest end of the room from the door. This is understandable because of the apprehension of certain meetings. However, being at the door greeting the membership is one of the most effective tools at setting a positive tone for the meeting.

The most significant benefit is addressing problems at the door and defusing these issues beforehand. It seems that some members will wait an entire year to come and complain about something that could have quickly been addressed in an email or phone call. While every issue cannot be caught, or every concern resolved, dealing with as much as possible at the door can help reduce negativity. Negativity tends to build upon itself at meetings, and it is more contagious than a cold.

The last benefit is simply a positive interaction with the membership. Unfortunately, the only interaction many members have with the board and association is receiving their dues payment coupons and covenant violation letters. Meeting a board member at the door puts a face on the matter. Even this limited personal contact at the door can help adjust the most negative perspective. It is difficult for most people, but not all people, to be harsh with someone who was being friendly with them a short time before the meeting.

Annual Meeting Guidelines

- After calling the meeting to order, advise membership that, "this annual meeting has been called to discuss the general business of the entire association. If you have any individual issues, please address these after the meeting with a board member or the manager. Also, you can complete a Homeowner Concerns Form and turn this in at the end of the meeting."

- Stand during the meeting. If standing during the meeting is not feasible, stand when addressing the membership.

- Have nothing, such as a table, between you and the membership during the meeting.

- Follow the agenda and do not discuss anything that is not addressed on the agenda.

- If conducting the meeting and someone speaks out of turn, call them down, and let them know he or she is out of order and there will be an open discussion at the end of the meeting. When people begin disrupting the meeting, it generally will only get worse if it is not addressed immediately.

- If someone continues to disrupt the meeting after repeated warnings, inform them that the meeting will be adjourned and will not proceed until he or she leaves. This should always be the very last resort.

- If there is a guest speaker, such as policemen, give them a time limit and advise them when they exceed this time limit. Guest speakers should not be inside the actual meeting. They need to speak before or after the meeting.

- When discussing detailed subjects, such as financials, always speak in general terms. If questions from the membership become too involved, defer these questions to after the meeting or invite these individuals to a board meeting to discuss in more detail.

- At the beginning of open discussion, remind everyone that, "this meeting has been called to discuss general business that affects the entire association. If you have any individual issues, please address these after the meeting or please request to be added to the agenda of the next board of directors' meeting. Or, please complete and turn in the Homeowner Concerns Form at the end of the meeting."

Chairing the Meeting

The Chair presides over the annual meeting or any deliberative assembly. The Chair can also be referred to as Chairperson, Chairman, Chairwoman, presiding officer, president, and moderator. The Chair conducts the meeting and is responsible for the orderly opening, progression, and completion of the meeting. In short, the Chair is responsible for the success of the meeting.

The specific Chair duties can include:

- Calls the meeting to order

- Along with the secretary, determines if the meeting quorum is achieved

- Announces the agenda items

- Allows recognition or assignment of the floor to members

- Enforces the rules of the assembly

- Asks for the second of all motions requiring a second

- Adjourns the meeting

The Chair should set the pace and the tone of the meeting. The meeting should be called to order on time and be adjourned at an efficient pace. This pace should adhere to the rules of the assembly and completion of the meeting objectives. However, the Chair must value everyone's time and be as efficient as possible. The tone of the meeting should be nothing less than business-like. Casual banter should be left for another time.

Key Points:

- The Chair shall follow the meeting agenda as written and shared with the membership; however, in the event an extenuating circumstance arises, then the Chair should ask and get permission from the assembly to adjust the agenda utilizing unanimous consent.

- The Chair runs the meeting. At appropriate points, such as officer and committee reports, the Chair asks for the officers and committee Chairman to speak.

- Allowing others to interrupt the meeting and have the floor can derail the entire meeting.

- Once the Chair relinquishes the floor, they should not interrupt a member who is following the rules of the assembly.

- In most instances, a member of the assembly must be recognized by the Chair before they can enter into debate or make a motion. For exceptions to this, please reference *Robert's Rules of Order*.

An Agenda with Sample Chair Talking Points

Annual Meeting of Happy Glen Homeowners Association

June 9, 2019

1. Call to Order - CHAIR: "I am John Smith, Chairman of this meeting, and at this time I would like to call the Happy Glen Homeowners Association annual meeting to order. If there are no ob-

jections, the agenda in your packet will be adopted." The Chair should pause and then say, "Since there are no objections, the motion is adopted. This annual meeting has been called to discuss the general business of the entire association. If you have any individual issues, please address these after the meeting with me, another board member or the association manager. We have a prescribed and limited agenda to adhere to, and there is an open discussion at the end of the meeting, so please hold any questions until that point in the agenda."

2. Introductions - CHAIR: "Again, I am John Smith, and I am president of the board of directors as well as the Chair tonight. Let me introduce the rest of the board of directors. Julie Smith is the vice president, Betty Jones is the secretary, Mike Jones is the treasurer, and Jill Smith is the member at large. I would also like to take a moment and recognize the members of our two standing committees, ARC and Pool. Our two ARC Committee members are Peter Smith and Kim Jones. Our three Pool Committee members are Jim Smith, Becky Smith, and Scott Jones. If anyone would like to help on one of these committees, there are sign-up sheets at the handout table."

3. Certify Quorum - CHAIR: Confirm with the Board Secretary that a quorum was achieved. Announce that, "We have a quorum."

4. Proof of Notice - CHAIR: Show Notice of Annual Meeting which is attached to the Affidavit of Mailing and state: "Proof of notice, if you did not receive this in the mail, please see the secretary or me before you leave so we can verify your address on the membership roll."

5. Review of Last Annual Meeting Minutes - CHAIR: "Please take a moment to review last year's annual meeting minutes that are in your annual meeting packet." (Allow time for the membership to read and move to the next item on the agenda) (The annual meeting minutes should be approved at the next board of directors'

meeting following the annual meeting. In the event there has not been a board of directors' meeting since the prior annual meeting, or possibly these annual meeting minutes have not been approved, ask the membership to read the minutes, and then state approved as read if there are no revisions. If there are revisions, then state approved as revised.)

6. Reports of Special Committees

7. Not necessary if no special committees, projects completed or underway.

8. Reports of Officers - CHAIR: "Again, we have a prescribed and limited agenda that we need to get through, and there is an open discussion at the end of the meeting, so please hold any questions until that point in the agenda."

9. President's Report - See President's Report Section of this book.

10. Treasurer's Report CHAIR: "I would like to introduce Mike Jones, treasurer, to give the treasurer's report." See Treasurer's Report Section of this book.

11. Elections - (Ideally the Chair should turn this part of the agenda over to a third party such as the Inspectors of the Election or the association manager. If the Chair is a candidate in the election, the Chair should turn this part of the agenda over to another party who is not a candidate or related to someone who a candidate) – CHAIR: "The Chair now turns the floor over to the Inspectors of election."

12. Nominations from Committee – INSPECTORS OF ELECTION: "Would the Nominating Committee give their report."

13. Nominations from Floor - INSPECTORS OF ELECTION: "Are there any nominations from the floor?" Close the floor for nominations after a reasonable amount of time.

14. Nominee Introductions - INSPECTORS OF ELECTION: "When I call your name would the nominees stand to speak and give their name, address, and tell why they wish to serve on the board of directors."

15. Voting - INSPECTORS OF ELECTION: "When completing your ballots, please write in the names of the candidates. Please remember, you can only vote for three candidates." (Allow a reasonable amount of time for everyone to complete their ballot) INSPECTORS OF ELECTION: "Has everyone completed filling out their ballot?" (Pause) "If so, please turn in all ballots at this time." (Allow time for all the ballots to be collected.) INSPECTORS OF ELECTION: "Do I have all the ballots?" (Pause) "If so, the polls are closed." (If there is not a completely independent inspectors of election, a good practice is to ask for two volunteers from the membership to count the ballots.) INSPECTORS OF ELECTION: "I would like to ask for two volunteers from the membership who are not running for the board of directors or related to anyone running for the board to help count ballots."

16. Election Results – The inspectors of election typically will announce the election results. It is best to avoid announcing vote totals unless pressed by the membership to do so.

17. Adjournment - CHAIR: "I want to thank everyone for attending tonight, and there will be a brief board organizational meeting after the open discussion. There is no more business on the agenda, so this annual meeting is adjourned." (The Chair makes a motion to adjourn the meeting. If the Chair had the agenda approved at the beginning of the meeting, the Chair need only state, "meeting adjourned.")

18. MEMBERSHIP OPEN DISCUSSION (Time Limit 3 Minutes) - CHAIR: "We have reached the open discussion portion, please limit your discussion to issues that relate to the entire association. If you have an individual issue, please address this after the meeting with me or another board member. You can also com-

plete the Homeowner Concerns Form and turn in as well. If you have a maintenance issue, there is a maintenance sign-up sheet at the handout table. Also, if you are interested, please don't forget to sign-up for any of the committees. And those committee sign-up sheets are also on the handout table."

Chairing Tips - Meeting Preparation

- Review minutes from last annual meeting. Make sure anything that was supposed to be addressed was addressed. If something was not accomplished, the Chair should be prepared to discuss. If a board member, association manager or another person needs to be able to discuss why something was not addressed, it is in the Chair's best interest to make sure this person is prepared to discuss.

- Review the agenda from the last annual meeting. Compare the upcoming meeting agenda to the last meeting agenda. Are there any material differences, are they significant? If they are significant, the Chair should be prepared to discuss with the assembly the differences and why. For example, moving the board of director elections to the top of the agenda to facilitate counting the ballots and have results before the end of the meeting.

- Review financials from the prior annual meeting. These should be compared to the financials that are going to be used at the upcoming annual meeting. Delinquencies, cash on hand and reserves can all be topics of conversation. Even with financials being the realm of the treasurer, it may be beneficial for the Chair to have a good understanding of these for the meeting.

- Review everyone's role at the annual meeting. Make sure that all board members know what is expected - for example, the secretary taking meeting minutes, the president and treasurer doing their reports, secretary and vice president assisting with and overseeing the sign-in or registration process.

- For potential contentious meetings, role playing the entire meeting is a good practice to help anticipate issues and how to deal with those issues.

Points that are Always in Order

- Point of Information: A request for information on a specific question, either about process or about the content of a motion.

- Point of Personal Privilege: A comment addressing a personal need - a direct response to a comment defaming one's character, a request to turn the air-conditioning down.

- Point of Order: A question about process, or objection and suggestion of alternative process. May include a request for the Chair to rule on a process.

Chairing Tips – For the Meeting

- The author cannot reiterate this enough: Do not deviate from the agenda, and do not take questions from the floor until open discussion.

- Stand and deliver. The Chair should remain on their feet throughout the meeting. The Chair may want to step to the side when others have the floor, but the Chair should remain standing. Standing is always, for lack of a better word, authoritative. The Chair must always be perceived as in control of the meeting.

- Even if there is a podium, the Chair should attempt to stand in front of the membership with no barriers. Barriers can effectively prevent the Chair from connecting with the membership. Barriers prevent the Chair from baring their soul.

- Arriving early gives the Chair time to acclimate to the environment. Running late or being rushed is never conducive to a Chair's presentation. Face-to-face interactions with members beforehand can build rapport that transitions into the meeting. These personal interactions may alleviate possible anxiety that the Chair may have for the upcoming meeting.

- Manage speakers and especially non-member speakers. Manage in two ways in particular: the time allotted to speak and, to whatever extent is possible, the speaker's topic. When the speaker is being scheduled, they should be advised of the time allotted for their presentation and be asked for a general outline of their talk. Two important aspects the Chair should keep in mind: a speaker drastically running over their allotted time to speak and a topic that causes controversy. Being forced to interrupt a guest speaker is never pleasant and best avoided by warning them upfront about time constraints. Second, controversial or potentially controversial topics can set the wrong tone for the rest of the meeting - for example, politicians coming to address a particular project that is affecting the association. In the author's experience, no matter the political party, or how much the politician assures everyone that their talk will not be partisanship, politics seems to creep into their talks. Another crucial point is that speakers should be outside the meeting, either before or after.

- Be positive as much as possible. Specific topics are going to arise that make being positive difficult, if not impossible, but the Chair having a positive demeanor translates to the audience, and hopefully, that is reciprocated.

Key Points

- The Chair controls the meeting.

- All remarks are addressed through the Chair.

- Members do not interrupt each other or the Chair.

- If a member is in order, the Chair does not interrupt a member.

Third Party Chairs

A board member, usually the board president, will many times Chair the annual meetings. However, there are many situations that appropriately call for a third party to perform this task. The most common is when the meeting has the potential of being highly contentious. A third-party Chair many times has the ability to take the emotional aspect out of the process, hopefully reducing the emotional aspects of all parties involved.

Another situation arises when the annual meeting procedural issues must be adhered to precisely. The author has experience with a retirement community, which has 5 or so former attorneys in the membership. This community's meetings are contentious, to say the least, and with these attorneys challenging every procedural process, it is quite the workout for the Chair.

Lastly, and probably the most common reason, the board simply wishes to have another party perform these duties. This can be because the board does not feel comfortable chairing the meeting, or they realize an experienced third party would be able to handle the task more effectively. No matter the reason, it is acceptable, and very common, for third parties to Chair homeowner association meetings.

In certain instances, an association's governing documents will have a provision stating the president should preside over all meetings of the membership or words to that effect. Parliamentary procedure allows deliberative assemblies to set aside rules such as this in certain circumstances. This process is known as "to suspend the rules." Suspending the rules can only be done at the meeting by unanimous consent or by a two-thirds vote of those in attendance. Suspending this rule is usually easily obtainable by unanimous consent. See section on unanimous consent.

If the association has retained an outside management company, ideally the association manager has the ability to perform the Chairperson task. If nothing else, the management company should have someone on staff that has been trained to chair meetings. There are situations when even if the management company has qualified personnel to serve as Chair, there still may be a need for an expert parliamentarian.

A parliamentarian is an expert on parliamentary procedure. Parliamentarians are many times attorneys, but not necessarily. Most major cities will have a law firm that specializes in homeowner association law, and these firms can be the best place to find a parliamentarian to chair an annual meeting.

When choosing a parliamentarian, or whomever to chair, make sure the person has actual experience of standing up in front of groups and chairing meetings. Chairing not only typically calm annual meetings but has experience chairing highly contentious annual meetings. Just because the person is an attorney, does not necessarily mean they have the ability or experience to perform the Chair function. The author attended a large and very contentious annual meeting in which an attorney was hired by the board to specifically Chair the meeting. When the board president asked him when he was going to call the meeting to order, the attorney informed him that he did not Chair meetings, that the "board president was required to Chair meetings." Notwithstanding the fact there were no such requirements for the board president to Chair the meeting, this author chaired the meeting while the attorney sat in the back of the room occupying himself with his cell phone.

Common Mistakes of Meeting Chairs

The most common mistakes meeting Chairs make:

- The Chair deviates from the agenda; thus, the Chair is "out of order."

- The Chair will give the floor to members during the meeting to ask questions.

- The Chair allows members to interrupt the meeting without calling them down and asking them to hold their questions until the end of the meeting.

Chairing a meeting is not a popularity contest; the Chair must maintain control or risk the meeting evolving into disorder.

To Suspend the Rules

Parliamentary procedure allows deliberative assemblies to set aside their established rules to do something that could not be done because of these preexisting rules. This process is referred to as "to suspend the rules." While there are rules that can be suspended, there are certain rules that cannot be suspended.

An association's governing documents are the "Rules" with regard to parliamentary procedure. The governing documents are established to protect the rights of individual association members and the right to carry out the will of the majority. Association members have a right to insist on compliance with any rules of the association; however, the membership at an assembly may dispense with certain rules.

Suspending rules are possible in the right situations. Usually, the purpose of doing this is to temporarily remove an impediment to nominal matters within the rules. For example, changing the order of business on a binding agenda to facilitate holding the board of director elections earlier on the agenda. With regard to association annual meetings, suspending the rules can only be done at the meeting by unanimous consent or by a vote of those in attendance.

In many instances, suspension of the rules can be accomplished by unanimous consent, also referred to as general consent. Unanimous consent is when no members of the assembly object to a procedure, such as the suspension of the rules. The principle that the rules are to protect the minority is thus waived when there are no objections from the minority.

To obtain unanimous consent, the Chair must ask if there are any objections to doing a particular procedure. For example, the Chair would say, "If there are no objections, the motion to suspend rules will be adopted." The Chair should pause and then say, "Since there are no objections, the motion is adopted." Since no member objected, the motion is thus adopted. If any member objects, the motion is not adopted and cannot be adopted without a formal vote of the those present. While in certain situations unanimous consent may be in order if the Chair assumes no member would object, in most cases it is best to formally ask if there are any objections.

If there is an objection from a member when unanimous consent is attempted, a vote of the membership must be taken to proceed with suspension. This is done by a motion to suspend the rules. If the motion receives a second, a vote of the members present, in person or by proxy, is taken. If two-thirds of those in attendance approve the suspension of rules, the rules are suspended. This motion to suspend is not debatable, amendable or up for consideration. This vote is typically done by a show of hands. If it appears that only one member is objecting, ask those objecting to raise their hands first. This will, many times, build momentum for the non-opposed to raise their hands in support.

Certain rules cannot be suspended: fundamental aspects of parliamentary law, issues requiring a vote by ballot, rules protecting individual member's rights and rights protecting non-present members of the assembly. For example, the quorum requirement could not be waived, or the meeting notice requirement could not be waived. Procedural rules established in state or federal statutes cannot be suspended. If a specific procedure is required or prohibited by statute, these rules cannot be suspended. Rules cannot be suspended simply because the rule is inconvenient, or even if the membership is unanimously in favor of suspension.

To suspend rules generally requires a two-thirds vote of the members in attendance. However, if the rule is protecting a minority of the membership of less than one-third, the rule cannot be suspended if there is opposition equal to the number of the minority members. A standing rule can be suspended by a majority vote of the members in attendance. Standing rules are established after the adoption of the bylaws, and these standing rules supplement and clarify certain bylaw provisions.

Sample Standing Rules for an Annual Meeting

1. All members must sign-in and register before entering the annual meeting room.

2. All members who wish to speak in open discussion must sign-in on the Open Discussion Speaking sheet.

3. Everyone – members as well as other attendees – are to be respectful of speakers. Silence cell phones, and refrain from using electronic devices during the meeting. Persons wishing to carry on conversations of more than a sentence or two shall move into the hallway.

4. Any member wishing to speak before the assembly shall rise and proceed to a microphone, and when recognized by the Chair, shall give his or her name and address before speaking.

5. All motions, discussions, debate, and reports must be addressed to the Chair.

6. A Member wishing to make a motion shall rise, and when recognized by the Chair, shall give his or her name and affiliation before presenting the motions.

---

7. Rules of Debate:

   a. Speakers will be limited to 3 minutes each and may not speak more than twice to the same motion. No person may speak more than once until all others wishing to speak to the motion have had an opportunity to speak at least once.

   b. At any time, debate may be further limited or extended by a two-thirds vote.

   c. The privilege of debate on the floor of the annual meeting is limited to Members of the association. Others may speak at the discretion of the Chair or with permission of the assembly.

   d. Only seated Members are eligible to make and second motions and to vote on matters put forth to the Member Assembly.

8. The rules contained in *Robert's Rules of Order, Newly Revised* shall govern this annual Member Assembly in all cases to which they are applicable and in which they are not inconsistent with the Bylaws and these Standing Rules.

9. The Chair is authorized to declare a recess of five, ten, or twenty minutes.

10. The Chair shall appoint a committee of three members to approve the minutes of the Annual Meeting.

CHAPTER SEVEN:
SPEAKING AT THE ANNUAL MEETING

"The secret of being a bore...is to tell everything"

– Voltaire

Speaking at the Annual Meeting

According to surveys, death is less feared than public speaking. Fortunately, successfully speaking at an annual meeting is achievable with preparation. Preparation is key to most things in life, and public speaking is no exception. Detailed below are key points:

Make brief notes or an outline of what is going to be discussed.

For example:

- Welcome and thank everyone for coming to the annual meeting. (Intro)

- New front entrance sign and flowers (1st topic)

- New clubhouse carpeting and painting (2nd topic)

- Plans for next year - tree trimming (3rd topic)

- Spring festival and the need for volunteers (4th topic)

- Thank everyone again for coming (Close)

An outline is a simple, straightforward and, most importantly, effective method of delivering a talk in an efficient and precise manner. The outline needs to be brief just to provide a "point of reference" to aid in the flow of the speaker's overall talk.

Never write out a talk. How people write is usually different from how people actually speak. Detailed discussion points, if memorized from written text and repeated, can come off as flat when delivered. Also, trying to remember written text can cause unneeded stress and cause the speaker to fumble.

Never memorize a talk word-for-word. A canned presentation is precisely that, a canned and boring talk. The end result is that the talk commonly comes off as robotic and monotonous. A memorized talk is often forgotten by the speaker just as they begin to speak.

Use examples in the talk. Giving an example or telling a brief story within the talk can make a presentation much more memorable. Examples of brief stories help the audience grasp certain points and help them focus during a talk. For instance, "A real estate agent was speaking with our association manager and told her that the new front entrance sign and flowers made a very positive impact on prospective buyers." Short and pointed examples can add color and provide recall to the listeners.

Be an expert in what is to be discussed. While the old adage "an expert is anyone from out of town" is humorous, serving on a board of directors makes a person an expert regarding the board's actions and considerations. The speaker should keep in mind that they probably know more than most of the membership about the particulars of the association. This fact should provide a level of confidence for the speaker's talk. The speaker should know enough about what they are going to speak about, so that their confidence and knowledge shine through.

Practice the talk over and over. - The old joke, "One day, after a rehearsal that had not gone well for legendary violinist Mischa Elman, he was exiting Carnegie Hall by the backstage entrance. Just then he was approached by two tourists looking for the hall's main entrance. Seeing his violin case, they asked, "How do you get to Carnegie Hall?" Without hesitation and continuing on his way, Elman simply replied, "Practice, Practice, Practice.""

Of all the points, practice is the key to a successful talk. For every 15 minutes of planned speaking, at a minimum, one hour of practice and preparation should be put forth. Practicing with other board members or family or even a mirror is time well spent.

"Practice does not make perfect. Only perfect practice makes perfect." - Coach Vince Lombardi

An important point to consider is that homeowner association members are not expecting a great and dynamic professional speaker chairing their meeting or speaking at their meeting. So, a slightly unpolished, but sincere, speaker is what is anticipated and in almost all cases accepted unconditionally by the membership.

An excellent public speaking tip is to find one smiling or pleasant looking person in the assembly to give the talk to. Do not give the talk to the crowd, find one kind or sympathetic face. Focusing on or thinking about the member in the front row frowning with their arms crossed can throw even the professional speaker off.

A speaker should never feel the need to tell everything they know. A brief overview in most circumstances is sufficient and appreciated by the listener. If more detail is desired the membership will ask during open discussion.

Speaking at Contentious Meetings

As the Chair, or as a board member, excess emotion is best left out of the dialog with the assembly. This goes for any personal observations that do not move the agenda forward. Moving the agenda forward to a successful conclusion is the ultimate objective. The Chair and the board have an obligation to the assembly to only conduct themselves in a way that accomplishes this objective professionally and proficiently.

While keeping excess emotions and unneeded personal observations out of the meeting may be easier said, then done, it is in everyone's best interest that this is accomplished. The Chair's responsibility is to maintain order at the annual meeting. Part of this maintaining order is to attempt to influence those board members and association members that may feel inspired to let their emotions get out of hand.

The author has found two effective methods of positively influencing individuals about their emotions. The first is speaking with the individual sometime before the meeting and going over whatever topic that has caused this spike in emotions. Many times, merely pointing this out to the individual that an annual meeting is not the place for unchecked emotions is sufficient. Possibly offering alternatives to this venue, such as the next board of directors' meeting. Sometimes, just acknowledging that the individual has a strong feeling towards someone or something and that you understand, can many times tamp the matter down.

The second method is the Chair asking the individual to assist them with preparing for the meeting and role-playing what is going to be said. This role-playing dialog sometimes alleviates the issue by either allowing the individual to vent or better analyze how they are coming across and not letting their emotions get the best of themselves.

Neither of these two methods will be 100% effective at tamping down all the many emotions that arise within every association. The success rate depends on the individual's personality and willingness to evaluate their emotions honestly. However, the Chair may find this tactic worth pursuing if feasible.

A number of years ago the author was asked, by two board members, to attend a meeting of a homeowner's association at a YMCA. The meeting was a combination of annual and special assessment meeting. The special assessment had suddenly electrified this upscale community that typically had a very carefree membership.

The two board members asked the author to speak with the board president and to offer his assistance with the meeting. Before the start of the meeting, the author had a long conversation with the president on the heightened level of emotions within the membership. The president was determined that he was going to make sure everyone in the room knew where he stood on the need for the special assessment. The author had several suggestions that were not well received by the board president except for one. The one being moving the board elections to the top of the agenda in the event the meeting had to be adjourned early. The president assured the author that an early adjournment was unlikely but considering that attendance was already at over 70% of the membership, moving the elections up would help facilitate counting all the ballots before the end of the meeting.

When the author entered the large and packed meeting room, there were no available chairs. It was standing room only, and there were more members standing than sitting. There is really no way to accurately describe the level of tension in the room. Except to say the tension was so think, a person could have levitated across the room.

The president called the meeting to order and moved the agenda to the election of directors. After the election was completed, he opened the floor for comments on the special assessment. With each question to the president, he was becoming obviously more frustrated and by all appearances was not attempting to conceal his contempt for the membership's questioning. After ten or so challenging questions, the president announced defiantly, "I want to let everyone know that the bylaws allow for the board to pass this special assessment without a vote of the membership and this meeting is just a courtesy!"

Well, to say the least, it was fortunate the board elections were held first, because the meeting went downhill from that point. Unchecked emotions can result in a meeting getting out of hand.

CHAPTER EIGHT:
THE AGENDA

Agenda

The agenda is the prescribed order of business to be addressed at the annual meeting. The foundation of an annual meeting is the agenda. Agenda formats can vary; probably the only constant is that an agenda begins with a 'Call to Order.' While the formats can vary, the mechanics are the same, or at least should be the same.

Almost all homeowner association meetings are conducted utilizing *Robert's Rules of Order*. State statute may even specifically require their use. While it may not be practical for most board members to become parliamentarians, obtaining a basic understanding of *Robert's Rules of Order* can be of significant benefit. Understanding the procedures for approving the agenda and moving association business efficiently can make the Chair's task much more successful.

Association governing documents, on occasion, can prescribe a specific agenda, or a binding agenda, to be used for their annual meeting. Some governing documents may require that an agenda be mailed along with the annual meeting notice. State statutes may have requirements regarding agendas and what must be included within the agenda. To ensure compliance, the association's documents and state statutes should be reviewed for specifics.

If the governing documents have any specific agenda requirements, these requirements should be adhered to by the prescribed process. That is, until the actual meeting where certain items can be appropriately circumvented. Circumvented, in an appropriate parliamentary procedure to improve the efficiency of the actual meeting. Not adhering to, or not correctly circumventing a requirement could negate the entire annual meeting. For example, a prescribed agenda is binding upon the assembly unless the rules are suspended. Simply introducing an agenda that does not conform to the binding agenda is out of order.

An agenda is not binding upon an assembly unless specified by the association's rules. The agenda could also be binding if it has been adopted for the meeting by unanimous consent, or by majority vote, at the beginning of the meeting. Nonbinding agendas are guidance for the meeting Chair, and do not necessarily have to be followed.

When an agenda is binding upon the assembly, the intention of the rule drafters was that this prescribed order of business be followed. Items cannot be taken up before their appointed place on the agenda. For example, in meetings where there are large membership turnouts, it can be desirable to move the election to the top of the agenda to allow for the additional time to count ballots. Strict adherence to a binding agenda would not allow this deviation.

To deviate from a binding agenda, the Chair should move to suspend the rules. The section: 'To Suspend the Rules,' goes into more detail on that process. The Chair could state, "I make a motion to suspend the rules and adopt the new agenda distributed, and if there are no objections, the motion will be adopted." The Chair should pause and then say, "Since there are no objections, the motion is adopted." Since no member objected, this motion is thus adopted. If any member objects, the motion is not adopted and cannot be adopted without a formal vote of the those present.

If there is an objection from a member when unanimous consent is attempted, a vote of the membership must be taken to proceed with suspension. This is done by a motion to suspend the rules. If the motion receives a second, a vote of the members present, in person or by proxy, is taken. If two-thirds of those in attendance approve the suspension of rules, the rules are suspended. This motion to suspend is not debatable, amendable or up for consideration. This vote is typically done by a show of hands.

If there is no binding agenda, the Chair should ask for general consent, or unanimous consent, to approve the agenda. If there are no objections, after a brief pause the Chair should proceed with the agenda. If there is an objection, the Chair then takes a vote of the membership and two-thirds is required to proceed with the agenda. It also allows for the Chair to simply adjourn the meeting when the agenda has been completed. These additional steps may seem unnecessary, but in a contentious meeting, taking the time to implement these steps can help facilitate a successful conclusion to the meeting.

Annual Meeting of Happy Glen Homeowners Association

June 9, 2019

Agenda

I.   **Call to Order**

II.   **Certify Quorum**

III. **Proof of Notice**

IV.   **Review of Last Annual Meeting Minutes**

V.   **Introductions of Board & Committee Members**

VI.   **Reports of Officers**

   A. President's Report

   B. Treasurer's Report

VII. **Elections**

   A. Nominations from Committee

   B. Nominations from Floor

C. Nominee Introductions

D. Voting

E. Election Results

VIII. Adjournment

Membership Open Discussion

Organizational Meeting: New and continuing board members will meet after the meeting to elect officers and establish board meeting dates and times.

Key Points:

-Place Open Discussion outside the meeting. Placing Open Discussion after adjournment prevents someone well versed in parliamentary procedure from having the floor and potentially disrupting the meeting.

-Minutes from an annual meeting should be approved at the next formal board of directors meeting. Or possibly, complied and approved by a committee especially formed to do so directly after the annual meeting. Procedurally, the assembly is reviewing the minutes from the prior annual meeting and not approving those minutes.

The President's Report

The president's report should revolve around what was accomplished in the prior year and what, if any, challenges that appear on the horizon. Thanking fellow board members and committee members is very appropriate. Many times, this is the only recognition board and committee members receive for their countless hours of volunteer service.

Hopefully, the president will have only positive items to report. If negative or controversial matters must be reported, the president should attempt to only relay the facts as they are, and not interject personal commentary. While this is many times difficult to accomplish, reporting just the facts always goes over best in these situations. Personal commentary or other observations about negative topics can have unintended consequences.

An example of a President's report:

First, I would like to thank everyone for attending tonight. I would like to thank my fellow board members for their service this past year. They all have spent a great deal of time in the performance of their responsibilities.

I would also like to thank the many volunteers and committee members. Their hard work keeps everyone's property values up and helps build a spirit of cooperation in our community. If you are interested in being on one of the committees, there are sign-up sheets at the hand-out table. This is important work, and it is safe to say the community could not operate without these dedicated people.

Now let me individually thank these people.

- The Architectural Review Committee: Bob Martin, Red Smith, Judy Smith, and Larry Pope.

- The Clubhouse Committee: Judy Smith and Leah Boloman

- The Pool Committee: Sally Sanchez, Linda Polhill, and Rich Presley

- The Landscape Committee: Mike Vicente, Jan and Jerry Oliver

- The Welcoming Committee: Mrs. Jenny Frances and Lewellen Cody

- Again, thank you all for your hard work! Please give them all a round of applause.

Accomplished & On-Going Projects

I am going to discuss the different projects that we worked on this past year and continue to work on. Again, please hold any discussion to the membership open discussion at the end of our meeting. We have a tight agenda, and we must get through it.

1. Sealing and re-striping the clubhouse parking lot. This came in under budget at $3,400. The original budget was $4,500. I think it looks great and is a drastic cost savings over repaving. Repaving would have been close to $50,000, and sealing gets us another 5 to 7 years.

2. The new pool furniture is in, and the Pool Committee spent a great deal of time on this project, researching and even visiting the manufacturer. I think they did a great job on their selection. This came in on budget at $21,250.

3. The retaining wall located on the east side of the Elm Road entrance that is being repaired has run into issues with road setbacks with the city. These delays should be resolved within the month, and we expect the repairs to still remain within budget of $22,000.

4. We have added three street lights on Redding Street where the walkway from the greenway trail enters our community. These three street lights cost, on average, a total of $125 a month combined.

5. We are having issues with the pool apron cracking, and we have concerns that these cracks could spread into the pool itself. We have contacted the company who constructed the swimming pool, as well as the community developer. With the pool being less than five years old, we are hoping we have recourse with the pool builder or the developer. We cannot discuss this in detail at this point, but we will be making everyone aware with a mailing in the next 60 to 90 days.

One more thing, Bob Martin is going to be stepping down from the ARC, so if you are interested in being on the ARC or any other committees, there are sign-up sheets at the handout table.

I will close with that. It has been an honor and pleasure serving as our community's president for the prior year. Thank you.

The Treasurer's Report

The treasurer's report should primarily revolve around the year-end financials and the financial situation since the last annual meeting, and if appropriate, any possible financial challenges on the horizon. Discussing capital reserves and that type of long-range planning financial matters are always a great topic to cover in this report.

The main consideration with a large group is that the report must be straightforward and void of complexities. Complex financial reports can be very challenging to explain effectively in a large meeting setting.

If collections are to be discussed in the report, this should only be done in a broad overview. Noting the increase or decrease in the collection percentages from the prior annual meeting goes a long way in addressing the matter. Too much detail can lead to membership questions about particular members who may be delinquent, which would not be appropriate to discuss because of possible collection statutes.

If the treasurer's report is going to be supplemented by handouts, these handouts should be very straightforward. An annual budget and balance sheet are generally the most common handouts. Income statements with multiple columns can be difficult to explain in this type of setting. An income statement with just the year-to-date income and expense column, along with the budgeted number for the items, are best for a large gathering. If someone would like a more detailed income statement, it is best to have a dozen or so on hand to distribute at the end of the meeting to those interested members.

An example of a Treasurer's report:

I would like to thank everyone for attending tonight. We had a good year, in terms of being on budget. We did have one exception, with an unexpected broken water pipe in the clubhouse that resulted in an expense to the community of close to $3,000. Our insurance policy has a five-thousand-dollar insurance deductible, so none of these expenses are recoverable.

Please look at our community's budget in the annual meeting packet. This budget reflects the 5% dues increase for this year. This increase went to pay for three primary expense categories: insurance, water, sewer, and electricity. These expenses increased the most of all our expenses this budget year.

Now please look at the 12/31 balance sheet in the annual meeting packet. Please note that paving reserves have increased from $5,000 last year to $21,115 this year. This increase is primarily due to the association's developer, HHU Corp, paying $20,000 to help fund this account. Hopefully, when the clubhouse parking lot has to be paved, we will have enough money built up.

The board of directors is currently seeking bids for a reserve study. There is a reserve study budgeted in this year's budget for $2,500.

Please see me after the meeting if anyone would like a copy of the annual audit and the detailed year-end income statement.

Thank you.

> **Key Point:** Keep the presentation simple. Complicated financial reports can be difficult to convey in a large meeting setting. If members wish for more financial details or other financial reports, this is better done one-on-one after the annual meeting.

Moving Elections to the Top of Agenda

There are a number of good reasons to move the election to the top of the agenda. The first usually being the necessity to finish counting ballots before the end of the meeting. This is especially the case with large membership votes. The next most common reason is a contentious meeting. If the annual meeting has the potential of being contentious, having the election before there is an opportunity for it to possibly get out of control can be a prudent move. A possible benefit of earlier elections for contentious assemblies is that voting may calm matters down. If an association has a prescribed agenda per their governing documents, see the section To Suspend the Rules.

CHAPTER NINE:
THE ELECTION

Elements of the Election

Parliamentary procedures can vary on particular elements of an assembly's election. An association's governing documents may have additional requirements that may be exclusive to the association. State statutes may have election requirements as well. These statutes could even conflict with accepted parliamentary procedure and the association's governing documents.

Most homeowner associations utilize the nomination from the floor process, which is also called an open nomination process. This procedure is used with most assemblies who elect their directors at an annual meeting. However, there are governing documents that address the nomination process through a nominating committee as well as nominations from the floor. There are also governing documents that only utilize the nominating committee process and do not provide provisions for floor nominations. What follows is a typical homeowner association annual meeting election.

Traditionally, the meeting Chair will turn the floor over to the inspectors of election, this being an independent party to conduct an impartial election. This is especially prudent or may be required by state statute if the Chair is a board member or a candidate in the election for the board.

The inspectors of election are, many times, appointed by the board of directors before the annual meeting. Governing documents, or state statute, may have specific requirements for inspectors as well. The inspector performs all the election procedures from opening the floor for nominations to announcing the election results. If there is not an independent inspectors of election, the association's management company will, in most instances, perform these duties as part of their service.

On the agenda, the board elections can be noted simply as "Elections" or broken into the different subsections. Typical subsections: Nominations from Committee, Nominations from Floor, Candidate Introductions, Voting, Election Results.

It is important that before the election portion has begun, the meeting Chair, or the inspectors of election, reviews with the assembly any candidate criteria typically found in the bylaws. Doing this beforehand can help avoid hurt feelings or other unpleasantness when it is discovered after the fact someone was disqualified from serving. An association's governing documents may have language requiring candidates for the board to meet certain criteria. Probably the most common is that the member be in good standing. There could be language limiting the number of consecutive terms that a member can serve. It is not unheard of to have language restricting convicted felons from serving. If the community has mixed forms of housing, there could be requirements for certain board positions to be held by members representing the different housing groups. Whatever possible criteria, before the election process is initiated is when this needs to be addressed before the assembly. If a member is elected, and it is discovered that they were not eligible in the first place, their election to the board would usually be null and void.

Nominations are typically for at-large positions on the board of directors. At-large director positions are open positions open to all nominees. Sometimes candidates are nominated for specific purposes or positions. If this is the case, this is an aspect of the voting that needs to be made exceptionally clear at the beginning of the election. For example, if certain director positions are intended for a style of home, and the director must reside in that style home.

Generally, all candidates for the election must be nominated from the floor. For example, if the association has a nominating committee, the chair of the nominating committee would officially nominate the committee's slate from the floor. If candidate names are submitted prior to the meeting, via committee or application, the inspectors of election should pose those candidates to the floor for nomination. For example, they may say, "The nominating committee has presented Mary Smith for nomination." Thus, Mary Smith is nominated from the floor. There are exceptions to floor nominations where the bylaws of an association require all nominations to go through the nominating committee and none are taken from the floor. Florida has enacted statutes to prevent this practice, no matter what the governing documents state.

Nominations do not have to be seconded. At this point, the inspectors of election solicit nominations directly from the floor. For example, they may ask, "Are there any further nominations from the floor?" If there are any additional nominations from the floor, the inspectors of election should repeat those nominees' names to the assembly and ask everyone to write the nominee's name on the ballot.

A member of the assembly does not have to be recognized to make a nomination. While nominations do not have to be seconded, if someone in the membership wishes to do so, it is acceptable and not out of order. Members can nominate themselves as well.

To close nominations does not necessarily require a motion to do so. The inspectors of election can simply close the floor for nominations when there are no further nominations. While the inspectors of election should be sure there are no further nominations, the inspector should also close nominations in a prudent manner. Prudent, meaning not to implore members to be nominated if there is no earnest desire in serving.

In the author's experience, it is best to avoid encouraging members who have no sincere desire to serve. This is even if there are not enough candidates for all the open board positions. Someone who has no sincere desire to serve will many times not represent the board well or fulfill their fiduciary obligations. At best, these indifferent new board members will fail to attend board meetings that could cause quorum issues. Everyone elected should have a sincere desire to serve on the board of directors.

There is a misconception, or more accurately an erroneous practice, of calling three times for nominations before closing the floor. While the inspectors of election should make reasonable attempts to ensure there are no further nominations, doing this is not necessary.

When nominations are being taken, the inspectors of election should be recording the names of the nominees. There are two reasons: first to provide a list of these names to the secretary taking the minutes, and the second reason is to recite the nominees' names back to the assembly.

Traditionally, once the floor has been closed for nominations, assemblies have board nominees introduce themselves; asking for a brief statement of why they wish to serve is many times a part of this introduction. The brief personal statements can be a huge determination of who is elected, thus should be encouraged. If a nominee is not present, the Chair can allow someone to speak on his or her behalf with the same time limit parameters used by the other nominees who are in attendance introducing themselves.

If a nominee is not going to be present for the election, typically a written affirmation from the nominee is required - an affirmation stating their willingness to serve. If this is a requirement, it should be noted as such in the annual meeting notice. For nominees in attendance, a verbal affirmation is acceptable and self-evident if they do not challenge their nomination and give a personal statement of their desire to serve to the assembly.

In many instances, these nominees' personal statements are the extent of what the assembly knows about the person. As a result, this is how many in the assembly base their vote. The author has witnessed nominees who made compelling personal statements and went on to make significant contributions to the community by their service.

The author has witnessed many nominees who made personal statements that essentially torpedoed their own election to the board of directors. The author Chaired an annual meeting in which a significant number of members were upset about a decision that the board had made a few months earlier. Of the hundred or so members in attendance, a large percentage were openly angry about the board's decision.

The leader of the largest hostile faction was nominated from the floor. When this leader began her personal statement about why she wished to serve on the board, she easily had more than half the room backing her for the board. She started her talk by brutally criticizing each board member in a personal and individual manner. She referred to how "stupid" the board members were and how she was "going to change things" once she was elected. This portion of her statement went on for around seven or eight minutes when she then began to attack the association manager. This attack was just as brutal as what she had dished out to the board.

At this point, the board president approached the author about calling time on her and shutting her down, as she had been talking for close to ten minutes by this point. When Chairing meetings, the author is always hesitant to call time on someone who has the floor who is not physically threatening members or using profanity. More telling was the more she spoke, the more the mood and tone shifted within the assembly. From the beginning of her personal and biting attacks on the board, her own supporter's body language and facial expressions were evolving. Her supporter's anger at the board of directors was turning to embarrassment and shock by their leader's uncouth behavior. Her supporters were looking down and turning away from her as she spoke; several of her supporters even left the meeting.

Not satisfied with just attacking the board and association manager, she began to single out other individual members and other groups within the homeowner association for her scorn. One group singled out were the members who were utilizing handicap parking spaces. She stated, "Most of these people look healthy enough to me and should be using regular parking spaces, and this will free up more parking spaces for the rest of us!"

After about fifteen minutes, members of the assembly were becoming tired of her behavior and started rumbling about how long she had been talking. At this point, time was called and the leader sat down. In the resulting election the "leader" received only one vote.

If the meeting facilities provide a whiteboard or easel with a writing pad, writing the nominees' names help facilitate the marking of ballots. It is essential to have clear and simple written and verbal instructions on how to mark ballots, and if available, written on the whiteboard. The inspectors of election should announce these instructions when voting begins. Complicated marking instructions or nonessential processes are prone to generate invalid ballots.

When a reasonable amount of time has been allowed for the members to mark their ballots, the inspectors of election should ask everyone for their marked ballots. After allowing time for everyone to turn in his or her ballot, the inspectors of election should ask, "Has everyone voted and turned in their ballot?" If there are no comments to the contrary, the inspectors of election should state, "The polls are closed."

Counting Ballots

The inspectors of election should make a last call for ballots. "Do I have all the ballots?" After a reasonable pause and if there are no objections, the inspector should state, "Since we have all the ballots, the poll is closed."

Ideally, the inspectors of election have no potential conflicts of interest regarding the association or an association member. However, this may not always be the case, such as with the association's management company or CPA firm who have contracts for services with the association. Part of this potential issue can be mitigated by seeking volunteers from the membership to assist in the counting of ballots. These volunteers from the membership, usually at least two, should not be running for or currently serving on the board, or related to anyone serving or running. Involving random member volunteers in this process can help alleviate the possible concern that something underhanded is going to be done while tabulating the ballots. It is not uncommon for non-conflicted inspectors of election to select volunteers to assist in the counting.

If feasible, the counting of ballots should be performed in the same room the annual meeting is being held. It would be ideal if this area is to the side of the room, so the membership would have the ability to observe, if so interested. If remaining in the meeting room is not feasible, allowing the candidates or others in the membership to observe the counting, if they so desire, should be allowed. However, these observers cannot participate in the counting or interrupt the tabulation process.

The counting of ballots should be done in teams of two, with one counting and one recording the totals on a tally sheet. Depending on the size of the homeowner association it may take more teams of two counting. Typically, the counting is done twice to verify the totals. Even if the winning candidate or candidates receive a drastically lopsided number of votes, verifying the total twice is a good practice. When all the valid ballots are counted and tallied, both volunteers should sign and date the tally sheet.

Countable and Uncountable Ballots

Reasonableness should be used in judging the validity of all cast ballots. If the voter's intent was discernible, the ballot should typically be counted. Issues can obviously arise in determining someone's intent.

If a member casts their vote for less than the number of candidates that they are eligible to vote for, the ballot is in most instances valid and should be counted. If a member votes for more candidates than they are eligible to vote for, the ballot is invalid or illegal.

Minor technical matters, such as not spelling the candidate's name correctly, would not necessarily invalidate the ballot if the voter's intent is obvious. Marking a ballot with a check mark instead of an "X" would not invalidate a ballot. Circling the candidate's names instead of indicating with a mark, as was instructed, would not invalidate the ballot if there are no other markings to indicate other intent.

Ballots cast for ineligible candidates, or fictitious individuals, are not valid and are deemed illegal or invalid votes. However, if a member had multiple choices on a ballot and cast a vote for a legitimate candidate and an ineligible candidate, the vote for the legitimate candidate would be counted. One ineligible selection on a ballot would not necessarily invalidate the entire ballot.

When ballots are ambiguous, or the intent cannot be easily discerned, these should be placed to the side during counting. Fortunately, most board elections are not so close as to hinge on one or two uncountable ballots. If the election hinges on the uncounted ballots, the inspectors of election can put the ballot in question before the assembly for determination.

Announcing Results

After the ballots have been totaled, the inspectors of election should compile an election report or list of results. The election report should list the candidates along with their corresponding vote totals. The candidates should be compiled in order of vote totals, with the candidate receiving the most votes at the top. All votes need to be accounted for on this report, even invalid votes such as ineligible candidates or fictitious individuals. These invalid votes need to be noted as such on the report.

At most homeowner association annual meetings, typically the election report is presented to the Chair. The Chair then announces who is elected to the assembly. Typically, the Chair only announces who was elected. If the assembly requests the vote totals, the Chair should provide the number of votes per candidate. This is even the totals for any ineligible candidates or fictitious individuals.

Inspectors of Election

Inspectors of Election are traditionally completely independent third parties to run an organization's board elections. While possibly not entirely independent of the homeowner association, it is common and acceptable for others to act in this role. Commonly, the association's management company representative, or other association professionals such as their attorney or CPA, can act in this capacity. If a member of the association serves in this role, the member should not be a current board member, a nominee for the board or have a close personal relationship with anyone who is running for the board or currently serving on the board.

Unlike most states, California's Davis-Stirling Act, has very specific language on inspectors of election. From those California statutes:

Independent Third Parties. As provided for in Civil Code §5110(b), inspectors may include the following:

-a volunteer poll worker with the county registrar of voters

-a licensee of the California Board of Accountancy

-a notary public

-a member of the association (who is NOT a member of the board of directors, a candidate for the board of directors, related to a member of the board of directors or a candidate for the board of directors).

Professional Inspectors of Election. There are companies that provide professional inspector services to associations. They can be hired to prepare ballots, mail and collect ballots and count votes. Putting an Inspector under contract does not violate the independent status of the Inspector. Civil Code §5110 provides that, "An independent third party may not be a person . . . who is currently employed or under contract to the association." As long as the Inspector is not currently employed by the association for other services, the board can hire the person to run the election.

Non-Independent Inspectors. There is another category of inspectors who are not truly independent, but typically define them as "independent" for purposes of the annual meeting elections. Examples are the association's CPA firm or management company.

Prohibited Inspectors. Associations may not appoint or use inspectors who are:

-members of the board of directors

-a candidate for the board of directors

-related to a member of the board of directors

There are professional firms that provide inspector services. These firms can prepare, mail and collect ballots. This service would also include tallying the collected ballots at the annual meeting. These professional inspectors of election firms are typically retained for public corporation stockholder meetings, especially when there is a possibility of litigation from stockholders.

The board of directors, in advance of the annual meeting, can appoint or hire the inspectors of election. An association's governing documents may require the board to appoint or form a committee for the inspectors of election. There could be exceptions to this in an association's governing documents in which the membership beforehand, or during the annual meeting, must vote to appoint the inspectors.

Surprisingly, while some governing documents may go into elaborate detail regarding inspectors of election, typically most governing documents barely touch on the topic, if at all. The duties and responsibilities of the inspectors of election can be specifically defined by an association's governing documents or state statutes. In general, these duties are:

- Ensure a quorum of the membership is present to hold a meeting and election.

- Determine the number of memberships entitled to vote and the voting power of each if voting is determined by percentage ownership.

- Verify the authenticity and validity of proxies.

- Open the floor for nominations.

- Close the floor for nominations.

- Hear and determine all challenges and questions to the voting process.

- Receive ballots.

- Determine when all ballots must be turned in.

- Coordinate the counting of ballots.

- Certify the election results.

- Ensure the election was conducted fairly for the benefit of the membership and in accordance with the association's governing documents and state statutes.

The Different Voting Methods

Typically, voting at most homeowner association annual meetings is done by utilizing written ballots. The use of ballots may be specifically prescribed in the governing documents, and state statutes may address ballot use as well. There are other forms of voting that may not be utilized as often or possibly not at all, but nonetheless, are relevant in certain situations. These are viva voce (voice vote), a rising vote, a show of hands, and a roll call vote.

Viva voce or Voice voting is the fastest and simplest method of voting. The meeting Chair will orally put the vote to the membership. First asking for those in favor to so indicate verbally, "yes," and then, asking those opposed to so indicate verbally, "no." The Chair will then decide the vote. Voice votes are generally used when there is an obvious majority agreement. For example, the association's bylaws require the membership to vote to approve the agenda for the annual meeting. Since there are generally no issues with an annual meeting agenda, a voice vote would be the most appropriate and efficient way to proceed.

Voice voting can be used for annual meeting board elections if the association's governing documents do not mandate ballot voting. Nominees must also be unanimous in support of voice voting. After the floor is closed for further nominations, the vote is taken on each nominee in the order of their nomination. However, in almost all instances, voice voting is not the best or preferred method for homeowner association board elections.

Rising votes are simply when the meeting Chair requests that members stand or rise for their vote. The Chair may decide the vote without counting those standing or may count the votes to determine the outcome. Rising votes are many times used when the Chair cannot determine the vote from voice voting.

Show of hands vote is as the name implies, a vote by raised hands. While this form of voting is often used in small gatherings, it can also be used in annual meetings of larger size. As with the prior two forms of voting, the Chair may decide vote outcome without counting the hands.

*Issues can arise with voice, rising, and hand votes with multiple owners of the same home voting. When this type of voting is utilized, the Chair needs to remind everyone in attendance of one vote per home.

Roll call vote is the process of voting in order of a member's name being called. While generally not utilized for homeowner association meetings, there are governing documents that specify this form of voting. This type of voting is generally limited to legislative bodies who are responsible to constituents.

Generally speaking, the membership at an annual meeting can decide on the voting method by adopting a motion on which method to utilize. However, voting methods may be specified in the association's governing documents or state statute. If this is the case, the association's attorney should be consulted on how to proceed if another method is preferred.

Secret Ballots

As with political elections, secret ballots are the most common form of voting for homeowner association board elections. Association governing documents and state statute may mandate a secret ballot. Even if an association's governing documents permit other forms of voting, state statute may take precedence and require their use.

There is an adage in real estate that maintains only three factors matter when buying: first, being location, second, being location and third, being location. When it comes to ballots, only three factors matter as well: simplicity, simplicity, and simplicity. The ballot should be easy to understand and easy to cast a vote.

The ballot can have preprinted names of candidates listed to aid in the selection process. These preprinted nominee names can come from nomination forms submitted beforehand or from the nominating committee. These can also come from current board members who have indicated they will be rerunning. Whether there are preprinted nominee names or not, there needs to be additional blank lines to write-in candidates nominated from the floor. Some state statutes may have specific requirements about names being preprinted on ballots, such as the names must be in alphabetical order.

Multipurpose ballots should be avoided. Multipurpose, being there are multiple issues other than the election of directors listed on the same ballot. For example, there is a vote for a special assessment or a vote on something other than the board election.

A single ballot may not be appropriate when there are multiple or different elections for the board being held - for example, a community with different style dwellings, such as single-family homes and townhomes, that have corresponding board positions. Governing documents may mandate that certain board positions be held by members residing in a particular style dwelling. In these instances, at membership sign-in, the different members should be given the corresponding ballot for their style of home. Combining multiple elections on one ballot can, at best, lead to confusion, and at worst lead to a contested election.

After the floor is closed for nominations and candidate introductions are completed, the inspectors of election should then instruct the assembly on how to mark the ballots, over-emphasizing how many positions are up for election and the maximum number for which members can vote. If a member requests a replacement ballot, the inspectors of election should provide a new ballot and have the member turn in their original. The inspector should void and sign the returned ballot and maintain for the election records.

It is a good practice to note the voting instructions on the ballot. For example, "You can vote for up to three candidates." The governing documents and state statutes could have specific requirements for ballot wording as well.

Ballots by Mail

Ballots by mail seem to be more prevalent in some regions of the country and with particular types of homeowner associations. This is most prevalent in vacation or resort areas where it can be more difficult to gather members together for an annual meeting. While voting by mail can be an effective method, it is fraught with details and is probably the easiest form of voting to contest. Associations many times shy away from this process because of the administration costs. Multiple mailings and material costs can easily quadruple the cost of a single meeting notice mailing. Another aspect other than the cost is that it can be a frustrating and expensive proposition if it is determined that some aspect of the mailing was not done correctly, and thus invalidates the entire election process.

First, the state statutes and the governing documents must be reviewed to ensure there are no prohibitions on ballots by mail, or possibly if there are any additional requirements that must be met. Guidance from the association's attorney should be sought to advise on any applicable statutes.

Nominations can be the most problematic aspect of ballots by mail. Problematic, in that the board of directors must make all reasonable attempts to ensure all interested members are given the opportunity to be nominated. Defining reasonable is akin to defining love, and this is where a board can unintentionally run into issues. Even if the governing documents have clear and specific guidance on this process, it is advisable to have the entire process reviewed by the association's attorney.

What follows is a typical ballot by mail process, but it is by no means a substitute for the association's attorney's guidance. First and foremost, the provisions in the governing documents addressing the nomination process must be followed. If there are no specific provisions on nominations, the board can draft a letter to the membership, asking members to run for the board and to have their name placed on the ballot. The letter should specify any requirements for serving, such as being in good standing. The letter should note the date of the meeting when the elections will be held and the number of open board positions. A nomination form should also be included in the mailing. Both the solicitation letter and the nomination form should indicate the date when the nomination must be returned by to be placed on the ballot by mail. The deadline to return completed forms must be reasonable, considering the delivery time of the initial mailing and the turnaround time. A thirty day or more response deadline is common. A mailing address to return the nominating form and other delivery options should be noted, if available, such as by fax or email. Some associations include a self-addressed, stamped envelope to help facilitate the ballot being returned.

Short biographies of themselves and their reason for wishing to serve should be encouraged to be returned along with their nomination form. This material will be mailed along with the ballot mailing. A limit on the amount of nominee information to be submitted must be established. If there is not a reasonable limit established, the re-mailing and copying expense may be excessive. The board should establish a set amount of space, or a word limit, to any biographical or campaigning material to be mailed. This established limit must be adhered to by all. If this limit is not adhered to, one candidate may believe another candidate received an unfair advantage.

Promptly at the beginning of the next business day after the due date, all the completed nomination forms should be compiled or certified as received by the board secretary or by the committee established for such purpose. For the association's records, this list of nominees should be signed and dated by two board members. The sequential mailing should be compiled as soon as possible. This mailing should include the annual meeting notice along with the ballots. Both the notice and the ballot should include wording to the effect. "To be counted, ballots must be received by the inspectors of election by the close of the election held at the annual meeting."

Governing documents, or state statute, may have requirements that all voting be done by secret ballot. If this is the case, the actual ballot should be free of anything that could be construed by the voter as a requirement to identify themselves. This could be something as innocuous as a line that could be mistaken for a signature line; therefore, a secret ballot must be free of signature, address places or space that could be construed as such.

Typically, how this secret ballot process is accomplished is similar to how municipalities process absentee ballots. The process involves three envelopes, a signature page or card and a ballot. The first envelope is for the initial mailing, along with two sequentially smaller envelopes. The larger of these two envelopes is self-addressed back to the association, and the last, smallest envelope is for the ballot. Note on this small envelope the following: "Ballot Only" and "Seal, place in self-addressed envelope." The signature card should have instructions on completing and returning the ballot, especially emphasizing the deadline for returning the ballot back to the association. Name, address, and signature make up the substance of the signature card. Some associations may require that the signature card be signed by a witness or witnesses attesting to the member's completing the ballot. The signature card should be too large to fit into the ballot envelope to avoid members placing the two together.

The returned envelopes, with the ballot envelope enclosed, should be presented to the inspectors of election at the meeting's election.

The inspectors of election should first open the envelopes and verify the signature card against the meeting's sign-in sheet. This is to ensure that no member who submitted a ballot by mail attended and received another ballot at sign-in. If members are not automatically mailed ballots, and they must be requested, this can also be addressed at sign-in by noting who was sent a ballot on the actual sign-in sheet. If there are any questions about a member receiving two ballots, that envelope and ballot envelope should be set aside and not counted until it is confirmed that the member only submitted one ballot. If an envelope is returned without a signature card or a properly completed signature card, the envelope and ballot envelope should be set aside as well, for later determination based on the standing rules of the voting by mail process.

The counting of ballots cast at the meeting should not be commenced until all the ballots by mail have been verified. At that point, the verified ballots by mail and the ballots cast at the meeting should be combined. Once combined, the ballots are to be tallied with no distinction as cast at the meeting or cast by mail.

There are methods to utilize ballots by mail in conjunction with a proxy by the member casting the ballot. This proxy is usually only used to help establish a quorum for the meeting. A proxy, in this form, is an item that the association's attorney should draft. Considering the individual state statutes regarding proxies and to comply with any requirements of a secret ballot, the association's attorney needs to draft an instrument that would be in compliance.

It cannot be stressed strongly enough that this entire process, voting by mail, should be reviewed by an attorney well versed in homeowner association law. If one step of this process is done improperly or deemed improper, the election could be deemed invalid.

Acclamation or By Acclamation

By acclamation, or unanimous consent is a form of election that does not use a ballot. This is an uncontested election. In the context of a homeowner association annual meeting election, it is most commonly used when there are more available board positions open than candidates running. Thus, these members are elected to the board of directors by acclamation. For example, there are three positions on the board open for election and only one person running. The one person running is elected by acclamation, since there is no need to use ballots.

An argument can be made if the governing documents require voting by secret ballot, and the documents do not make exceptions for uncontested elections. If the Chair does not obtain unanimous consent from the assembly, ballots should be cast and counted to make a formal determination.

If vote totals are needed to make other determinations, this can be a factor in necessitating a formal ballot vote. For example, if vote totals are required to determine length of board term. This most often happens at transition time from developer to membership control, when a board will have staggered terms going forward.

Percentage Ownership

Percentage of ownership is the basis of a member's ownership, typically in a condominium. This percentage typically determines dues amounts and voting rights. There are occasional exceptions to this where dues are based on percentage interest and every member has an equal vote. How the initial property developer determines the percentage of ownership for each unit can vary from development to development. This percentage ownership is typically established in the declarations of covenants when the association is first formed.

A condominium project would use a uniform formula or method to calculate percentage ownership. This formula is typically based on the intrinsic value of the unit, as it relates to the value of the entire association. This formula can be based on many different factors: square footage, number of bedrooms, number of bathrooms, location in the building and other aspects that can be calculated into the value of the unit.

These percentage of ownership calculations are generally found in the appendix of the declarations of covenants of the condominium. This appendix schedule or table will many times specifically correspond percentage ownership to each individual unit. The total percentage of ownership of all the units should total 100% or thereabouts of the entire association.

If an association is built in different phases, the percentage ownership will change with these additions to the association. The declaration of covenant's appendix will be amended by the association developer to reflect the change in percentage ownership, reducing the prior member's ownership percentage and including the new construction to, once again, a total 100% of the entire association.

Example of percentage ownership language found in governing documents.

Section 5.6 - Voting Rights: The total number of votes of the Association Membership shall be equal to the total number of square feet of Building space contained within the Building from time to time, and each Member shall be entitled to one (1) vote multiplied by the number of square feet of such Member's Unit; provided, however, if fee simple title to any particular Unit is owned of record by more than one person or entity, all such persons or entities shall be Members of the Association, but the vote with respect to any such jointly owned Unit shall be cast as hereinafter provided in this Section 5.6. The number of square feet of each Unit is set forth on Exhibit B of the Declaration.

Key Points - Percentage Ownership at the Annual Meeting

-Noting the member's percentage ownership on the sign-in sheet beforehand will speed the sign-in and ballot distribution process.

-Counting ballots that are based on percentage ownership can be challenging, especially with large associations with more than just a few percentage classifications. Using colored paper ballots for the different classifications can help speed calculations.

-There are many thoughts and opinions on how a tally sheet for percentage ownership ballots should be structured. The author has found the most efficient to be a simple matrix: with the candidates' names listed across the top of the sheet and the percentage ownership listed in a column down the left side. See Appendix for an example of this tally matrix.

Cumulative Voting

Cumulative voting is a form of voting that is intended to strengthen the ability of a smaller voting block to use all their votes to elect a candidate or possible candidates. Cumulative voting allows members to cast all their votes for a single candidate for the board of directors when there are multiple positions open. For example, there are three openings on the board of directors, and instead of voting for all three, the member places three checks beside one candidate's name.

Governing documents can specifically allow cumulative voting or disallow its use. It is very common for cumulative voting not to be addressed at all in an association's governing documents. If this is the case, state statutes dealing with nonprofit corporations, or possible specific homeowner association statutes, would need to be reviewed for guidance.

The one key point regarding cumulative voting: if the governing documents or state statutes allow, the membership must all be made aware of this form of voting. Insofar as cumulative voting is allowed, and members are utilizing this form of voting, everyone must have the opportunity to vote using this method. If cumulative votes are going to be accepted and counted, this must be announced at the beginning of the election.

Voting Certificate

If issues arise about which owner from a home has the authority to vote at an annual meeting, a Voting Certificate may be useful in this determination. This certificate can be utilized for legal entities in which it is difficult to determine a party who represents the entity. Governing documents may have other voter certification requirements. If voting certificates are to be utilized, they typically need to be on file before the annual meeting. See the Appendix for an example of a Voting Certificate.

Runoff Elections

Runoff elections are not a common occurrence in most homeowner association election processes. These usually happen because of a tie vote or a material error during the election process. Generally, a runoff election cannot be held at the same meeting where the initial tie vote or error occurred. The runoff being another election, a special meeting for this purpose would need to be held. This special meeting would typically need to be noticed to the membership in accordance with the notice requirements of an annual meeting.

Contested Elections & Record Retention

On occasion, an association will have a contested election or at least questions about the results. While not very common, some associations will have written rules or policies on ballot retention and other points regarding contesting an election. State statutes may have retention requirements as well. California's Davis Sterling Act mandates that ballots be retained for one year from the date of the election.

Notwithstanding any state statute or governing document requirement, an association can adopt rules dealing with a member contesting an election. These rules may specify how long a member has to contest an election and how long the association will maintain ballots. These rules would generally need to be adopted before an actual election to be utilized for that election.

If the ballot count is challenged after the adjournment of the meeting, the board should establish rules on how this recount is to be done. Most importantly, who will be present to perform and witness the recount. Usually, the association secretary would be tapped for this duty unless they were a candidate in the election being contested. Someone contesting the election should never be allowed to be alone with the ballots. If there is a challenge to the election during the actual meeting, this can be addressed with *Robert's Rules of Order*.

In the event of litigation, all the election records should be maintained until the association's attorney advises otherwise. Even if the association has not been served with a lawsuit but has a reasonable belief that a matter may result in litigation, records should not be destroyed.

CHAPTER TEN:
OPEN DISCUSSION

Open Discussion "Unhappy Member"

Four Points

The term "Unhappy Member" is used for lack of a better word and should not necessarily be perceived as negative, because not everyone who is being overly vocal should be viewed in a negative or unproductive context. Many members voicing their concerns at an open discussion can provide valuable input and feedback. A great deal can be learned from others and their experiences.

With all this being said, there are some in the membership whose sole purpose is to criticize and add nothing productive to the conversation. Dealing with certain individuals, such as this, can be a challenge to the Chair, board and even the rest of the membership. There are four important points to consider when dealing with an unhappy member.

First and foremost, the Chair or board should never take anything personally. Now, realizing that this can be easier said than done, the critical point is that emotions never lead to productive and effective retorts. When the Chair or a board member responds in a less than calm manner, this can benefit the unhappy member in that they can gain credibility. This credibility may develop if the membership interprets this defensiveness from the Chair or the board member as an indication that the unhappy member is correct.

Second, listen intently to what is being said. Members can believe they are not being heard. If appropriate, ask for the members' ideas or their solution to the problem. If the unhappy member is sincere in their views and honestly wants a solution, they may offer valuable input. If the unhappy member has no practical solutions, this will put their remarks in the right context with the rest of the membership.

Third, tell the truth. While obviously always a good practice, sidestepping around an issue or shading an issue in most cases can make a situation worse. However, there are many instances where a board will want to manage their information. Pointing out additional factors that have no real bearing on the matter can give the unhappy member more ammunition.

Fourth and probably most importantly, responses should be directed to the entire membership. Meaning, trying to convince one unhappy member of anything can be difficult, if not impossible in certain situations. Winning over the majority of the membership is, in many instances, much more feasible. In most cases, the membership is on the board's side, or at worst has neutral feelings towards the board. Unhappy members usually represent far less than 5% of the assembly and in many instances only one or two members. So, the lesson here is to focus on the members who can be converted and not the ones who are unyielding.

If these four points fail to gain traction, there is no burden on the Chair or others to respond. Many times, it is appropriate to thank the unhappy member for their input and move to the next member. Unfortunately, there are certain instances that "thank you" is not appropriate, and the only proper response is, "Next person."

Let 'Em Talk

In governmental assemblies, speakers are traditionally allotted three minutes to speak. Associations, being quasi-governmental assemblies, usually follow this same standard. However, there is generally no requirement that three minutes must be strictly adhered to. The Chair generally has a great deal of leeway with allowing members to speak in open discussion.

With this being said, it is very common for speakers, during open discussion, to verbally attack the Chair, board of directors, and others in the membership. So much so, that this attack can become very uncomfortable for everyone who bears witness to the onslaught.

Another common reaction is for the board or the Chair to shut the speaker down even before their three minutes is up. Shutting a speaker down is usually a mistake unless the speaker is utilizing profanity or physically threatening others. Even if the speaker is verbally abusing the board and stating claims that are false, it may be best to let the speaker run their course.

It is important to consider that the vast majority of the membership came to the meeting to learn about what has been happening within the community. Most members are intelligent and rational enough to see through nonsense or rhetoric. This is especially true if the speaker is allowed to talk for an extended period of time. In most instances, the speaker will begin digging a hole that will be impossible to climb out of. The author has witnessed countless speakers who started speaking with a substantial number of "followers" in attendance. With few exceptions, the speaker usually tended to turn not only the rest of the membership against them but in many cases, alienate their own followers. The key factor is to always let the speaker talk as long as they wish. Typically, the membership will begin protesting when they feel they have heard enough out of the speaker. The Chair should avoid shutting a speaker down because it may be perceived that the board has something to hide from a speaker talking.

If the speaker says anything that is incorrect, or the Chair or board of directors wish to challenge what was said, by all means, do this, but the let the speaker finish. Again, the speaker will normally sink their own ship without the board having to intervene.

Of course, in the event that the speaker is stating something which is correct and there is no defense, it may be best to not offer a defense. Most people can accept the fact that boards make mistakes. However, most people have little tolerance for personal shortcomings, such as trying to deflect or blame others for their mistakes.

The author was present at an annual meeting open discussion when a very articulate member proceeded to totally eviscerate the board president and the rest of the board of directors. The best description of her technique would be: savagely brutal in a professional and pointed manner. This member never raised her voice, but her tone and delivery were akin to an attorney cross-examining a hostile witness, multiplied by ten. One of the board members commented afterwards, that she thought Hannibal Lecter had eaten his sister. The severe dressing down was the result of a decision that the board had made. The board had no real defense other than they just made a poor decision. Upon completion of the extremely brutal dressing down, the board president stood and responded by simply stating, "Yes, we made a bad decision, and we are all sorry that it turned out the way it did, and if we had it to do all over again, we would not make the same decision." He then sat back down. There was a long awkward pause, and Hannibal Lecter's sister appeared to be at a loss for words, but finally responded with, "Well everybody makes mistakes." And then she sat down.

The Solid Gold Podium

While a breakdown tabletop podium does not have to be made of gold, it is worth its weight in gold. A common issue with open discussion and annual meetings, in general, is members who have a negative perspective on the homeowner's association. As a matter of fact, these types of people have a negative view on most everything.

Unfortunately, negativity is as contagious as the flu and as detrimental to a meeting where successfully completing the agenda is the ultimate goal. Many times, this negativity is to stir up resentment within the community for no legitimate purpose other than to sow discontent. A great tool to deal with this negativity is a podium at the front of the room. If members wish to come up and run down the association, they can come to the front of the room to do so.

The author has been to hundreds of annual meetings, and without fail, it is always someone sitting on the back row in the assembly who feels the need to spread their form of sunshine. Rarely, if ever, is the input from this member conducive to any practical solutions. More often than not, it is only conducive to fermenting discord amongst the membership and the board of directors.

It is important to realize that open discussions are for matters affecting the entire membership, so facing the membership is in accordance with this open discussion process. The member is directing remarks to the entire membership, not just to the board of directors.

A board or the Chair should never want to censure or prevent members from voicing legitimate concerns. However, if the member feels so strongly about a topic, coming to the front of the room and directly facing everyone should not be an onerous task.

Certain members will gleefully stand in the back of the room and throw bombs, but when it comes to actually having to face their fellow members, the bombs have a propensity to not be thrown. The author has witnessed the hardest of hearts melt when having to face fellow members. Of course, there are exceptions as some members are happy to spew discord anywhere and everywhere.

A breakdown tabletop podium costs around $100 and is money well spent if the meeting location does not provide a podium.

Speaking Sign-Up Sheet

While most governing documents are silent on the requirement of speakers at the annual meeting needing to sign-up to speak, it is a practice with some associations. A sign-up to speak sheet should have a place for the person to put name, address, and what they wish to talk about. This sign-up sheet should be left out during the entire meeting, and members should be allowed to sign-up at any time throughout the meeting.

A sign-up to speak sheet is not a method to reduce the number of speakers, but a method to improve efficiency and to help maintain order. The practice has one primary administrative benefit in that if the secretary wishes to note who spoke in the open discussion, this makes that task easier.

There are five practical benefits of this sign-up to speak sheet as well. First, the speakers are generally better prepared to speak and are more efficient with what they have to say. Second, the act of having to sign-up reaffirms that the members are to talk at the conclusion of the meeting and not interrupt the meeting. Third, it allows the Chair to call members up to the podium and establishes the podium as the proper place for the members to speak during open discussion. Fourth, if the topic the person wishes to discuss is of an individual nature, the Chair can ask the member to complete the Homeowner Concern Form or speak with a board member afterwards. Fifth, having members state what they wish to speak about prevents or reduces steamrolling. Steamrolling is the tendency of a speaker to build upon the intensity of a prior speaker. By having speakers talk about different topics in the order they signed up in, the numerical order, helps prevent a speaker from complaining about the same topic and attempting to outdo the intensity of the prior speaker.

A Homeowner Concerns Form

An excellent tool for annual meetings is the Homeowner Concerns Form. There is an example of this form in the Appendix. This form has two practical purposes. First, it reduces members wishing to speak at open discussion about matters of an individual nature, such as a neighbor dispute. This form can be mentioned when the Chair at the beginning of open discussion announces that only issues affecting the entire association should be discussed. Thus, providing those members with individual issues an alternative to open discussion. Second, this form is a benefit to those members who are reluctant to speak in front of the membership for whatever reason.

CHAPTER ELEVEN:
CONTENTIOUS MEETINGS

Contentious Meetings

The two primary reasons annual meetings go off the rails:

1. The Chair taking questions during the meeting and not waiting until open discussion.

2. The Chair or a board member losing control of their emotions.

Out of Control Meetings

A homeowner association annual meeting, being a deliberate assembly, has the right to enforce the meeting rules of decorum. At all meetings, each member should be expected to act politely and professionally to other association members and the meeting Chair.

At one time or another, almost all homeowner associations have had issues with disruptive members during an annual meeting. While not ideal, a deliberative assembly has the right to admonish members whose behavior is objectionable. Fortunately, there are effective methods of dealing with disruptive members.

At the beginning of the meeting, the Chair should announce the following:

"The governing documents of our association have established the procedures for how the meeting is to be held. There is an established agenda as dictated by in our association's governing documents. Because of this, please do not interrupt the meeting unless you are addressed by the Chairman of the annual meeting.

Please note at the bottom of the agenda that there is an open floor discussion session which allows the membership to voice issues of a nature that involve and relate to the entire membership."

No matter the situation, the Chair must remain calm and never lose their composure. In emotionally charged meetings, not losing composure can be a herculean task. This is, in many instances, where third-party Chairs (not a member of the association) are utilized to significant effect. Third-party Chairs should not have the emotional baggage that would be carried by a member of the association, because when the Chair loses their composure they can lose creditably of the assembly.

The main concern with a member becoming disruptive may not necessarily be that member, but the members who follow the example in this member's unacceptable behavior. Disruptive members beget more disruptive members. For whatever reason, people become emboldened when they see others not being held accountable.

The Chair is responsible for addressing disruptive behavior. Depending on the severity of the disruption, the Chair should first call down a disruptive member as being out of order. For example, the Chair would state, "Sir you are out of order, please refrain from interrupting the meeting. There will be an open discussion at the end of the agenda where you can address your concerns." The Chair should use their best judgment in deciding to escalate these warnings if the member repeats the same offense. If appropriate, the Chair could escalate their warning with: "Sir, I have advised you once not to interrupt the meeting. If you interrupt the meeting again, I will ask you to leave the meeting." When the level of expulsion is reached, the Chair must be resolute in their words, and if the member continues in their actions, they must be asked to leave. With this being said, expulsion should be the very last resort to restore order to the meeting.

One nominal method of escalating a warning to a disruptive member is to ask the secretary to note this member's behavior in the minutes. For example, "I am going to ask the secretary to note your behavior in the meeting minutes if you continue to be out of order." Many times, this is ineffectual because a member may not mind that their behavior is going to be noted in the minutes. However, on occasion, this does work and may be worth attempting.

Ejection of a disruptive member from a meeting is proper procedure per *Robert's Rules of Order* and an inherent right of any deliberate assembly. A deliberative assembly has the authority to determine who may be present during a meeting. This authority is derived from the assembly's rules, or by a vote of the assembly's membership. If ejection of a member is determined to be in order, the meeting Chair is required to enforce the rule of order.

However an ejection is accomplished, no greater force can be used than necessary to perform the task. If physical force is utilized, the homeowner association and anyone involved in the removal could be subject to legal liabilities from the person ejected. Fortunately, ejecting a member from an annual meeting is not that common; however, the Chair should always be prepared to do so. Failing to remove a disruptive member can jeopardize the cohesion and stability of the meeting.

If a member refuses to leave when asked to leave, ideally the police should be contacted. The Chair can call a temporary recess until the police arrive. Depending on the meeting venue, removing the disruptive member may not be possible. Certain public facilities, such as libraries, may not permit people to be removed. If this is the case, the only option may be for the Chair to adjourn the meeting until such a time and place where order can be restored. Again, ejecting a member from the assembly should be the very last resort.

If the Chair is unable to deal effectively with a disruptive member or multiple disruptive members, many times the only course of action is to adjourn the meeting. Unfortunately, shutting down the meeting is often the goal of the disruptive members. Sometimes meetings are so contentious it can be almost impossible for the Chair to keep control of the meeting. As mentioned in other sections of this book, the two fastest ways for the Chair to lose control of a meeting is deviate from the agenda and to take questions from the floor before open discussion.

If a disruptive member is anticipated beforehand, a plan could possibly be established to preempt this disruption. Before the meeting, an intermediary could attempt to resolve the matter, or at least let the member know they are being listened to which may placate the matter. During the meeting, this designee, someone other than the Chair, can attempt to get the disruptive member to the side and attempt to address their concerns. It is always preferable to avoid potentially embarrassing someone by calling them down or possibly ejecting them from the meeting. An intermediary, many times, can prevent these embarrassing situations from happening.

There are two factors the Chair must always have in the forefront. First, the Chair must control the meeting. Losing control of the meeting can, at best, waste time and, at worst, shut the meeting down completely. Second, the fact that most of the meeting attendees did not come to have another member disrupt the meeting. Disruptions are not considerate to the other members of the assembly.

If a member must be asked to leave the assembly before the elections, if feasible, the member should be given the opportunity to cast a ballot. While situations may make this impractical, by providing the member the opportunity to vote, he cannot claim he was disenfranchised. Of course, if he is being disruptive in the meeting and being removed because of this behavior, disenfranchisement may be a difficult point to argue.

Abusive behavior, such as the use of profanity or threats to other members, is grounds for immediate removal from the meeting.

Security

While fortunately, having security or police officers attend annual meetings is generally not a common occurrence, on occasion, it can be a necessity. There are several points to keep in mind when the need for security arises.

In many municipalities, the local law enforcement agency will assign a police officer to a community as a "Community Police Officer." The intention of this direct representation is for the officer to have a closer relationship with the community, and put a face on law enforcement. Associations commonly invite this officer to their annual meeting to speak and introduce themselves to the membership. The author is aware of associations who have had such good relationships with their community police officer that the officer would come and speak and stay for the entire meeting.

Having the community police officer present can be beneficial in many instances, and if they can stay for the entire meeting, this can be beneficial as well. Issues can arise with paying the officer to come as security for the meeting, while they are also coming in their capacity of community police officer. In some circumstances, hiring another off-duty officer to come and provide security may be prudent.

An important point to consider: If someone becomes disruptive, will the venue allow for that person to be removed? Many public buildings, such as libraries, have policies that prevent people from being removed. Many times, as long as the member is not being physically confrontational, there is no way to extract them from the meeting.

The author has a colleague who was chairing an annual meeting in a library several years ago. Halfway through the meeting an extremely large homeless man, well over 6 feet tall, suddenly stormed into the meeting room screaming. What could be construed from his screaming was that the "devil was after him and he was going to kill everyone in the room." What was most

challenging for everyone to understand was if the homeless man meant he was going to kill everyone in the room or that he was warning everyone that the devil was going to kill everyone in the room.

What made the situation even more problematic was that the annual meeting was for a senior community of people 55 years and up. With the average age in the room being in the high sixties and predominantly female along with some attendees in wheelchairs, my colleague was in quite a predicament.

To say the least, the screaming homeless man got everyone's undivided attention. He had no connection with the association and had just been wandering around the library when he decided his participation in the meeting was warranted. The police were called, and upon searching him, there were no weapons found. The police then took him outside the library and released him. Several minutes later he came back into the meeting room and calmly sat down on the front row. In all the years my colleague has been attending and Chairing annual meetings, this was the first time that no one wished to speak during open discussion, so the meeting was adjourned early.

A Pre-Meeting Meeting

A pre-meeting meeting or a dry-run meeting or an agenda-setting meeting, whatever name that appeals to the membership, may be the right tactic to calm the waters. This is a general membership meeting called by the board of directors just before an annual meeting, typically a week or less. These meetings are less formal. Generally, it is not necessary to track the membership or meet quorum, and they are used typically to address a contentious issue that has erupted within the association.

The rationale behind this type of meeting is that it is a good method to try to tamp down a fire in the community before the annual meeting. At first thought, some would look at this and say one awful meeting is enough, why have two awful meetings. Surprisingly, this first meeting many times has a calming effect on the annual meeting. This is not to say that these pre-meeting meetings are a walk in the park, but they do tend to make the annual meeting go smoother than anticipated. For whatever reason, possibly everyone got everything off his or her chest at the first meeting, or perhaps the attendees are still tired from the first meeting, pre-meetings have been effective. While a pre-meeting may not be appropriate in all situations, it may be worth considering if a very contentious matter is afoot within the homeowner association. This can also be an opportunity to collect proxies for the upcoming annual meeting if members are unable to attend.

CHAPTER TWELVE:
IMPROVING MEETING ATTENDANCE

How to Improve Annual
Meeting Attendance

Annual Meeting Date

In many instances, the date or possibly the time of year of the annual meeting is predetermined in the association's governing documents. The date of the annual meeting may coincide with the time the declarant transitioned the association to membership control. The author, from experience, has found the least favorable months for attendance are December, July, June, November, and August. These months coincide with holidays and when members are on vacation or concerned with other more pressing matters. The most favorable months for attendance are March, April, February, and January, in that order.

The day of the week affects annual meeting attendance as well. The best days of the week for attendance are Tuesday, Thursday, Monday, and Wednesday, in that order. Weeks that include a public holiday are best avoided because of the inclination of people to take additional time off around holidays.

Notice Period

Notice period refers to when an annual meeting notice must be mailed to give legal notice to the membership. The notice period is usually specified in the association's bylaws. The wording will generally be similar to this: ...notice shall be delivered not less than ten (10) nor more than sixty (60) days before the date of any such membership meeting... Annual meeting notices must be placed in the mail during the prescribed time period, but picking the optimum amount of lead time can be hit and miss. Ideally, the 15 to 20-day notice allows members to plan ahead for the meeting, while not so far ahead that members forget. A postcard mailer, reminding the members of the meeting and timed to arrive in their mailbox 1 to 2 days before the meeting, is very effective. Email or text blasts the day before and the day of the meeting are very effective methods as well.

Pitney Bowes, a manufacturer of mailing equipment, conducted a survey on mailing trends from direct marketers. They were asked which was the most responsive day of the week for their mailings, and Tuesday was selected overwhelmingly. While this is presumably based on solicitations and their related follow-up, this is still a good indication that people may pay more attention to their mail on Tuesdays. From the author's experience, mail arriving on Tuesday, Wednesday or Thursday does garner more attention than the other mail delivery days.

Recognition & Awards

Recognizing committee members or other people in the membership is an effective method to improve attendance. While in most cases these types of active members will be in attendance, these active members, many times, have a following that will attract other members to see them receive recognition. This recognition does not necessarily need to be tangible, but having members stand up for applause goes a long way.

Short & Efficient Meeting

When members can anticipate an hour or so for a meeting that runs smoothly, attendance is generally better. It should be obvious that long and tedious meetings are detrimental to attendance; however, this is commonly overlooked. The real benefit of these efficient meetings is that a more representative group of the membership are present. Representative, in that more members tend to come with a positive outlook to learn what has been achieved and how the association is moving forward. Long and tedious meetings tend to attract a higher percentage of members who are in attendance that seem to have an ax to grind. Long and tedious has never seemed to deter ax-grinding members.

Captivating Meetings

While captivating may not be the typical word one hears in describing an annual meeting, a meeting can be interesting or raise the membership's curiosity enough so that they attend. Discussions affecting the association, such as a local municipality service change or a development on a neighboring property, are common interest topics that can draw members to the meeting.

It is important to notice these discussion topics or guest speakers on the annual meeting notice, or better yet, noticing this on a separate sheet of paper to make sure it stands out in the mailing. If the meeting agenda is mailed along with the notice, included items such as this may be overlooked in all the other mailed material.

Guest speakers are a common method to attract more membership participation, and the right guest speaker can add a great deal to the meeting, while the wrong guest speaker can have the opposite effect. The first and most oblivious question: Is there a very strong reason to have a guest speaker? The guest speaker's talk must add significantly to the meeting and benefit the entire association before this is even considered. The association's community police officer is a common membership draw because members are interested in crime and crime prevention within the community. It is advisable to have the speaker outside the official meeting, before the call to order or after adjournment. There are procedural issues with this, and this prevents meetings from becoming bogged down with questions of the speaker. No matter the speaker, the Chair should establish time limits to ensure the speaker's talk does not impede the meeting.

Orderly Meetings

Keeping order may seem like an obvious point, but the board must realize the ramifications of a disorderly meeting. Disorderly and contentious meetings result in less membership attendance. Which only makes sense because people typically do not seek out stressful contentious environments.

CHAPTER THIRTEEN:
ADDITIONAL MEETING POINTS

Member in Good Standing

The topic of members in "Good Standing" usually only comes up once a year, and that is usually at the annual meeting. Not being in good standing typically revolves around three aspects of a member's obligation to the association: delinquent in paying their assessments, in violation of the governing documents or in litigation with the homeowner association.

Governing documents may have provisions addressing a member in good standing and what constitutes that status. Many times, these provisions will specifically restrict members who are not in good standing from participating in the annual meeting. To determine whether the association can suspend a member's privileges, the bylaws are the first governing document to review. The heading or term may vary from the governing documents of one association to another; however, "Member in Good Standing," is probably the most utilized term. What follows would be considered a good example:

Section 4.1. MEMBER IN GOOD STANDING. A Member shall be considered to be a "Member in Good Standing" if such Member:

a. Has, at least ten days prior to the taking of any vote by the association, fully paid all assessments or other charges levied by the association, as such assessments or charges are provided for hereunder;

b. Is not in litigation with the association;

c. Has discharged all other obligations to the association as may be required of Members hereunder, or under the association documents.

The Board shall have sole authority for determining the good standing status of any Member at any time and shall make such determination with respect to all Members prior to a vote being taken by the Association on any matter. The Board shall have the right and authority, in its sole discretion, to waive the ten-day prior payment requirement if extenuating circumstances exist. Any Member not conforming with the provisions of this Section 4.1 shall be declared by the Board to not be a Member in Good Standing and shall not be entitled to vote on matters before the Association, hold a position on the board of directors or utilize any of the Association's amenities until such time Member in Good Standing status is attained and so declared by the Board.

While the above example is very detailed, some association's bylaws may offer sparser language, or possibly not have any provisions regarding this topic.

Unfortunately, the term "good standing" is ambiguous and has no legal meaning or basis. Typically meaning unless there is very specific governing document language that supports sanctions against a member not in good standing, enforcement of these sanctions can be problematic.

When the language of members in good standing is vague, or does not offer enough detail, the association's attorney should be consulted. If the governing documents fail to address this issue, amending these documents may be a viable option. The association's attorney should be consulted on amending governing documents as well. If governing document language is void of member in good standing language, state statutes may offer remedies to address this issue.

Even when the association's governing documents have specific language addressing a member's good standing, state statutes need to be reviewed. State statutes could possibly require additional steps that must be taken or possibly forbid any action being taken. For example, in North Carolina, depending on when an association was legally formed, if the documents have the good standing language, a hearing is required. This hearing is to be in front of the board of directors before any member's rights can be suspended or curtailed.

No matter the status of a member, in good standing or not, they still must be notified of the annual meeting. Members not in good standing may have the right to attend membership meetings, but not participate. It is a common practice for members not in good standing to be mailed, along with the annual meeting notice, a course of action of how they can improve their standing.

Guest Speakers

Having guest speakers at an annual meeting is very common, and possibly much too common. The right guest speaker can add a great deal to the meeting, while the wrong guest speaker can have the opposite effect. The first, and the most obvious, question is if there's a very strong reason to have a guest speaker. The guest speaker's talk must add significantly to the meeting and benefit the entire association.

Potentially controversial speakers may even need to be cleared by the association's attorney. An example of this would be the former homeowner association developer wishing to speak to the membership to discuss issues that could lead to litigation. Controversial speakers can set a tone for the rest of the meeting, good or bad, and usually bad.

Politicians are frequent guest speakers, and usually the most controversial. Even if the politician is coming to speak about a specific project or matter relating directly to the association, these talks are, in most instances, controversial. For some reason, no matter the Chair's request and the politician's assurances that the talk will be nonpartisan, it always seems to be partisan to some degree. It may be that politicians honestly believe what they say is nonpartisan, or possibly they do not care if it comes across as partisan. The ramifications of controversial talks can linger long after the annual meeting and many years to come. In most instances, controversial speakers should be avoided, or possibly regulated to speaking to just the board of directors at a board meeting.

No matter the topic, the board of directors and the meeting Chair should have a good understanding of what will be discussed by any speaker. Allowing someone to address the membership without having at least an overview of the talk can be a recipe for problems. Consequently, by allowing someone to address the membership, the board could be perceived as condoning or endorsing whatever is said.

The meeting Chair should establish time limits for the speaker's talk. The Chair should determine if and when the speaker will answer questions. The Chair could relegate questions to the speaker after the meeting or if questions should be directed in another medium, such as by email or talking with the speaker outside the meeting room.

The most crucial point when having a guest speaker is to have this talk outside the official annual meeting. This can be accomplished by having them speak before or after the actual meeting. Because of procedural issues, it is advisable to keep a strict business-like agenda that does not get bogged down with a guest speaker and any related questions from the membership.

Taking Meeting Minutes

Minutes must be taken for the annual meeting. The board secretary traditionally takes these minutes. These minutes should be approved at the next formal meeting of the board of directors. In the event there is no formal board meeting between annual meetings, the minutes would be approved at the following annual meeting or by a board es-tablished committee specifically formed to perform this task.

Minutes are the written record of the meeting maintained by the secretary of the association. Minutes document decisions made during the meeting and provide an official record of any actions taken. Minutes are not a word-for-word transcription of everything that is said. Minutes should state what was accomplished, rather than denote every detail of the meeting's discussion. Generally speaking, an entire annual meeting's business should fit on one, or possibly two typed pages.

The Basic Content of Meeting Minutes:

- Association Name

- Specific Meeting Type: Annual

- Date

- Location of meeting (legal address)

- Time meeting called to order

- Note that meeting quorum was established

- Names of board members in attendance

- Precise wording of every adopted motion

- Notations of failed or withdrawn motions

- Name of the person who made the motion

- Name of the person who seconded the motion

- Election: Who was nominated and the vote outcome

- Committee reports given

- Time of adjournment

If the membership open discussion is held within the meeting, any written statements from members should generally not be included or attached to the minutes.

Post Annual Meeting Steps

The board secretary or the association manager should obtain all the board members' contact information, emails, phone numbers, and mailing addresses.

The board secretary or the association manager should email everyone's contact information to the entire board.

Record Retention: sign-in sheets, proxies, nominating applications, marked ballots, and proof of notice of meeting. These items should be maintained by the association's secretary or management company. A copy of what was distributed, e.g.; the meeting informational packet, should be maintained in the official records as well.

State statute or possibly governing documents may have additional record retention requirements. There may also be statutes regarding posting new board members names or notifying the membership via other methods.

Records Retention

It is not uncommon for association boards to establish a resolution regarding record retention, especially for an annual meeting and the election supporting documentation. These resolutions will typically provide a 90-day period where the membership can contest an election; after that, the ballots and supporting paperwork are destroyed.

Resolutions such as this are implemented for a number of reasons, and the most common is probably long-term storage practicality. Another common reason is concern that a contentious member or members will attempt to disrupt the operation of the board of directors by continually challenging the election. While the last reason is understandable, normally this concern is unfounded. Because if a member or members are going to be disruptive, they are still going to be disruptive even if the ballots are destroyed or maintained.

Resolutions of this type need to be implemented well before an election to avoid any appearances of impropriety. If implemented after the meeting, the optics can be less than ideal. The exception being that an assembly may establish a rule stating that after the election results are announced, ballots will be maintained for a certain period and then destroyed. Thus, giving the membership notice, and if they wish, to contest the results. There may be record retention requirements in an association's governing documents that must be followed, as well as in state statutes.

At a minimum, the approved minutes of the annual meeting should be maintained in the permanent records of the association. A copy of the agenda, along with any items distributed to the membership, are generally appropriate for the permanent records. Items or attachments that a member of the assembly would like added to the minutes, or included in the permanent files, are usually not appropriate.

In the event of litigation, all the election records should be maintained until the association's attorney advises otherwise. Even if the association has not been served with a lawsuit, but has a reasonable belief that a matter may result in litigation, records should not be destroyed. Destroying records can result in court sanctions that can jeopardize the association's legal position.

Virtual Meetings

There are numerous technologies in existence that allow members to "attend" an annual meeting without physically being present. Telephone being the oldest, and Skype, Facetime or Google Hangouts being the most recent medium. It is becoming more common for public corporations to have virtual annual meetings. This may be because Delaware has statutes that provide for virtual meetings, and over half of all Fortune 500 companies are Delaware corporations. Of these companies, the majority are utilizing audio-only meetings.

The common argument for virtual meetings is that it will improve membership participation. The reasoning being that the meeting will be more convenient for the membership and possibly more efficient operationally. The possible convenience is easily discernible, while being more efficient operationally can be another matter. If virtual attendance can be used for the quorum calculation, this may be the case; however, setting up the systems and the related costs may offset any operational efficiencies.

Virtual meetings are most commonly held in conjunction with a traditional annual meeting. Attempting to hold a virtual-only meeting without the membership in attendance could violate the association's governing documents or state statute. Even if a virtual meeting is permissible, this may not bode well with the membership, who are accustomed to a traditional meeting.

A common question is: Can members attending virtually be counted towards the quorum, and can they vote remotely? Even if state statutes permit virtual meetings, two factors typically come into question. First, will the virtual attendees be able to actively participate in the meeting? Second, since there is not a sign-in sheet, how to verify membership remotely or virtually.

While verifying membership virtually may be achievable with live video feed, audio-only meetings can make this verification challenging. Participation would generally entail members being able to vote remotely and speak during open discussion. Voting brings up a number of issues, ranging from secret ballot requirements to verification and cost of possibly hiring an outside service to perform the polling. All these many aspects make contesting a virtual meeting much easier to do than a traditional meeting.

Technical problems can play a part in disrupting a virtual meeting. These types of issues could possibly lead to the meeting and election being contested. This would be based on a member claiming that they were affected by a technical glitch and could not participate.

In the author's experience the homeowner associations that do virtual meetings most successfully do so only as a convenience to the membership who cannot attend. Virtual meetings are popular with resort area associations that have many absentee members who may have to travel to attend. This convenience being that the virtual attendees are not counted towards quorum and virtual voting is not offered. In these situations, with nonparticipating members, the annual meeting notice should specify that voting and open discussion will only be available for members in attendance physically. To alleviate this, it could be noted that questions can be submitted to the board beforehand to be answered during open discussion. Indicating voting options, such as ballot by mail, or designating their proxy to a member in attendance is advised if they cannot attend. The only drawback to this type of nonparticipating virtual meeting is that it may reduce attendance if members elect not to attend, who would normally participate. This reduction in physical attendance may endanger meeting the quorum requirement.

Whatever form of virtual meeting that a board elects to do, the association's attorney should review every aspect. This review would be for participating and nonparticipating virtual meetings. Compliance with the association's governing documents and state statute should not be taken lightly when it comes to ensuring a properly run and valid annual meeting.

Declarant Control Period

The declarant control period is the period of time before the association is turned over to the membership's control from the declarant. The declarant, also commonly referred to as the developer, is the person or entity that organizes the homeowners' association.

Generally, at the end of the declarant control period, or near that end, the declarant calls a formal meeting of the association membership in which members are elected to the board of directors. The declarant may or may not be involved any longer in the association. State statutes regarding declarant and homeowner associations can vary drastically on responsibilities and the exiting of homeowner association developments.

Annual meetings under declarant control can be a difficult topic to summarize for many reasons, again primarily because of the different state statutes. Compounding this difficulty in summarizing is when there are no state statutes addressing declarant control. Therefore, the association's governing documents and possibly case law are the only resources. Consequently, we are forced to generalize here, and specific points may have to be gleaned from other sources.

The Declarant and the Annual Meeting

When it comes to the association declarant and their role in the association, for lack of a better phrase - they call the shots. This is also, many times, the case concerning the annual meeting and control of the board of directors. Frequently, the board of directors are either employees of the declarant, or family members of the declarant or possibly the declarant is a one-person board, serving as all the officers.

Whatever the state statute or governing documents dictate, usually the declarant has control through the phases of construction, or how many homes are built or left to be developed. Control may also be dictated by a future turnover date as outlined in the association's governing documents. It can also be a combination of both these build-out or future date factors. Other factors could play into this control period and the exit of the declarant.

Super-voting rights are typically how the declarant maintains control of the board of directors. The declarant and the association members will be classified as a certain class of membership within the association. What follows is typical of language found in governing documents.

Example of this Document Language

Class A Membership

Class A members are designated as owners of homes and have one (1) vote for each lot owned.

Class B Membership

Class B membership is designated to the declarant, who is allowed up to three (3) votes for each home or lot held by the declarant. Class B membership is pursuant to the declarant's ownership of lots or homes that are subject to assessments. Class B membership automatically converts to Class A membership when either 90% of the authorized residential homes or lots transfer to the membership or 25 years from the date of the filing of the declarations of covenants of the community.

There are instances when the declarant is required to intermittently, or at specific points during the development, add nonaffiliated association members to the board of directors. Many times, the declarant can appoint these members. There can be requirements that allow these nonaffiliated members to be elected directly from the membership by vote at an annual or a special meeting called for this specific purpose.

One common denominator of all associations, even during the declarant control period, is that annual meetings must still be held. Even if there are no board elections, the declarant must still call and hold an annual meeting. The declarant generally has the same duties and obligations as a membership-controlled board of directors.

CHAPTER FOURTEEN: DIRECTORS & OFFICERS

The Difference between a Director and an Officer

Members may serve on a board of directors for many years and not realize there is a difference between a director and an officer. In short, an individual is elected as just a director in most instances to serve on the association board of directors. After the election, these directors convene amongst themselves to select the officers.

The definition of an association director is an individual acting on behalf of the membership of an association. A director is responsible, along with other members of the board of directors, for overseeing the operation of the homeowners' association, and thus protecting the property values of the membership.

Directors have a fiduciary responsibility to the association membership in the exercise of their duties. Directors have the authority, as granted in the association's governing documents and state statutes, if applicable, to hire and discharge vendors, call meetings of the membership, and determine other matters affecting the association.

Depending on the association's governing documents, directors may or may not be members of the association, and may or may not have to be in "good standing" to serve on the board of directors. Generally, being in "good standing" means that the member is not in litigation with the association or is not past due with their association assessment payments.

The directors, or more precisely the board of directors, elect the officers. The association's officers typically consist of a president, vice president, secretary and treasurer. On occasion, governing documents may provide for other officers, such as chairman in lieu of the president's position or a sergeant at arms position. On an association board of directors, officers have specific roles and duties regarding the operations of the association. Governing documents, generally the bylaws, specify the officer positions that are to be filled. Officers' duties vary by position and may be specified in the governing documents, but the primary responsibility of the officers is the operation of the association.

The Role of the President

The role of the association president is broad in scope and can be difficult to pigeonhole. The ultimate goal of any board of directors is to increase the overall standard of living of the membership and to increase the value of the property within the association. The president is charged with leading this effort.

- The president is tasked with working closely with the other board members, association manager and membership to determine the overall goals of the association.

- The president must have a good understanding of the association's governing documents.

- In the broad view, the president is responsible for the association's fiscal well-being. This includes collecting assessments, guiding the budget process and making sure that reserves are adequately funded.

- The president is charged with making sure there is adequate insurance coverage to protect the association from liability and other hazards.

- The president finds and develops potential volunteers and future association leaders.

- The president maintains close working relationships with the association manager and other association vendors to make certain of the efficient operation of the association.

- The president presides at board meetings and other association meetings. The president prepares meeting agendas and makes certain that proper voting procedures are used.

- The president must not necessarily be a great public speaker, but the president is the representative of the association and must be an effective communicator.

Establishing Goals and Priorities

The president helps establish association goals, and these goals help direct board efforts. The president should also prioritize these goals, and thus, provide a framework for these being accomplished. Clearly-defined goals contribute to the success of the association. Goals can range from "we will lengthen the pool season and pay for it by..." to "we will retain an engineering firm to perform a reserve study."

Association Governance

Association presidents are required to interpret and carry out many association governing tasks, such as preparing meeting agendas and conducting meetings. Presidents are also charged with working with the various association committees.

The Association Representative

Being the highest office of the board, the president speaks officially for the board of directors and the association. The president usually serves as the liaison between the board and the association manager. An important point a president must remember is: when speaking on behalf of the association, he or she must report back to the board on what has been said. The president's communications and decisions must be in line with the views of the board.

Working with the Board

The president must have a spirit of cooperation when working with the board, which many times will have varying opinions and ideas. The president should encourage the other board members to participate because the contributions of board members are vital.

Forming Committees

Because of the many actions and topics at any given board meeting, the board cannot always handle all the work in an effective manner. When this occurs, committees can provide an important service to the board of directors and the president.

Committees can focus efforts on topics that need in-depth research, input, and thoughtful consideration before a recommendation is made. As an added benefit, committees provide an opportunity for the membership to participate. With board guidance, the president is tasked with appointing committee chairs and explaining the committees' tasks. The president should also establish time frames for committee reports. Once the committee is established, the president should be available to provide additional guidance.

Fiduciary Responsibilities

The president must put forth more effort than other board members, with regard to fiduciary responsibilities, because the president's role can be more extensive regarding negotiating contracts with vendors and dealing with the association manager. Board members and the general membership trust that the president will act in the best interests of the association when performing their duties. However, the president does not have authority to act without board guidance or consent.

Board Meetings

The president is responsible for conducting efficient board meetings that attend to the matters of the association. Board meetings are for conducting association business and decision-making. The president should always review the association's governing documents for specific meeting guidelines. In general, to conduct an efficient meeting the president should:

- Prepare a timed agenda and distribute it well in advance of the meeting.

- Come to the meeting prepared and insist that the other participants be prepared as well.

- Take charge. Tell the board members the topics for discussion and how the meeting will proceed.

- Have a good understanding of *Robert's Rules of Order* and use them to conduct an orderly, efficient meeting.

- Stick to the timed agenda. Meeting participants know what to expect when the president follows the written agenda.

- Keep the agenda moving and be considerate of the time constraints of the meeting.

- Focus discussion on the issues at hand and the information that the board members received prior to the meeting.

- Remain businesslike and calm. To effectively manage the meeting, the president must conduct the meeting in a way that promotes a pleasant and efficient meeting.

- Approach issues in an impartial manner.

- Always remember that everyone on the board is a volunteer and that their time is valuable. An efficient meeting can be completed in an hour rather than in hours.

The Agenda

At least several days before the board meeting, the president should prepare an agenda and distribute it to the board. Supporting documentation, as it relates to the items on the agenda - i.e., treasurer's report, a president's or manager's report, minutes from the previous meeting and other documents should be included with the agenda into a board packet. The board packet should lay out the details and create the groundwork for the issues at hand to be discussed. An organized and specific-timed agenda allows the board to work much more efficiently. A tight-timed agenda keeps discussion of issues and actions moving efficiently.

The Agenda Should:

- Set a time limit for the length of the meeting and discussion of each agenda item. This keeps board members focused and moving towards a decision.

- Include a descriptive sentence on topics to clarify issues. An action statement of the needed motion helps identify what is needed to move the issue along. An action statement might read, "We have been asked to allow grills on the clubhouse patio, but the association manager recommends that we not approve because of fire hazard concerns." This type of action statement is more to the point and is results-oriented.

- Prepare motions before the meeting. The president should state the motions on the agenda that are expected to be made. Action statements help direct the discussion and make decision-making easier.

An added benefit is that it also makes it easier to document motions in the meeting minutes.

- List new business on the agenda. Always eliminate any surprises at the board meeting - no decision should be made on issues presented that are not on the agenda beforehand.

- There is an old saying that "no business is old business," but it can be unfinished business. Any action delayed by the board from a prior board meeting can be listed as an agenda item.

The Role of the Vice President

The role of the association vice president can be wide in scope, as is the president's, but can also be narrow in scope, depending upon the vice president or the board of directors. The vice president may assume additional duties as defined by the board of directors and the association's governing documents.

The vice president is charged with all the powers required to perform the duties of the association president in the absence of the president. The vice president does not possess innate powers or authority to act in the capacity of the association president. Generally, the vice president may only act for the president when the president is physically absent or otherwise unable to act.

Establishing Goals and Priorities:

The vice president works very closely with the president in establishing association goals for the future. As the second position in the association leadership chain-of-command, the vice president, many times, helps the president prioritize the association's goals.

Council to the President:

In most cases, the vice president works very closely with the president of the association and provides needed input. In this role, the vice president provides a "sounding board" for the president and thus helps define issues.

Committee Leadership:

The vice president, many times, will take additional leadership roles and will chair committees. Because of the significant time commitments on the architectural control committee and the landscaping committee, the vice president will preside over one of these committees. Chairing these committees is a great way to prepare for broader leadership roles.

Leadership Development:

The vice president, along with the president, finds and develops potential volunteers and future association leaders.

The Role of the Secretary

The role of the association secretary may be easier to define than that of the association president or vice president, but it is no less varied. Whereas the association president is charged with leading the association, the association secretary is charged with maintaining the records and protecting the association from liability.

The secretary records meeting minutes and board resolutions. The secretary affixes the association's corporate seal to legal documents and verifies the signatures on those documents. The secretary verifies the proxies for the association's annual meeting or any special meetings of the association. The secretary is charged with maintaining all the association's records and distributing accordingly.

Duties of the Secretary:

The association secretary's duties are classified into three job functions: recording secretary, corresponding secretary, and filing secretary. Recording secretary, as it implies, is the taking of minutes and the recording of corporate resolutions. Corresponding secretary is the function of sending notices as required by the governing documents of the association. The filing secretary is the function of maintaining all the records of the association and disposing of old records.

Recording Secretary:

The recording function is taking meeting minutes, drawing up resolutions, making sure the minutes are approved and distributing approved minutes.

Taking Minutes:

Meeting minutes are vital for the documentation of association business; however, there are many misconceptions about what minutes should contain and not contain. Minutes are definitely not a detailed transcription of what was discussed. Minutes should reflect what was accomplished only.

Resolutions:

A resolution is a determination of policy of the association by the vote of its board of directors. Resolutions are often statements of policy, belief or appreciation and do not supersede or amend the association's governing documents. For example, a bank may require a resolution for a loan stating that the association has the authority to take out a loan.

The resolution has three parts: authority, reason, and extent. For example: Whereas the association's governing documents give authority to the board of directors to take out loans from financial institutions - from time to time - in order to meet the needs of the association; now, therefore, be it resolved that a loan be taken out for an irrigation system for the beautification of the association. It is also resolved that the loan will be for no more than $100,000 and with a repayment term of no more than 60 months.

Approved Minutes:

When meeting minutes are approved, the meeting's presiding officer (board president/chair, vice president, and so on) and secretary should sign and date. Once this step is accomplished, the minutes are approved and finalized. These original meeting minutes should be placed in the association minute book. In some instances, copies are forwarded to the association's attorney for legal review or compliance.

Corresponding Secretary:

The corresponding secretary is ultimately responsible for all communications to the membership: this includes annual and board meeting notifications and any other correspondence from the association. The actual tasks of generating and mailing are generally delegated to the property management company or agent.

Filing Secretary:

The secretary keeps the official association minute book where the association's meeting minutes, corporate resolutions, proceedings and board of director and membership votes are maintained. The secretary maintains an owner's list with corresponding mailing addresses. The association, being a legal entity, must always maintain the records in compliance with state statutes. The files should also be kept in a manner so as to defend the association in the event of a legal action. The following are typical items that are maintained in the association's permanent files: meeting minutes, articles of incorporation, bylaws, CC&Rs, amendments, blueprints, surveys, plats, financial statements and vendor contracts.

The Role of the Treasurer

The treasurer is the financial voice of the board of directors and the association. The role of the association treasurer can be narrow in focus and is crucial to the smooth operation of any association. Whereas the association president is charged with leading the association, the treasurer is charged with ensuring the financial wellbeing of the association.

The treasurer's responsibilities are usually specifically spelled out in the association's bylaws. Generally, the treasurer has the overall responsibility for the association's funds and securities and is responsible for keeping full and accurate financial records. This does not necessarily mean the treasurer physically has to perform accounting tasks, but ensure they are being done.

Duties of the Treasurer:

The primary responsibilities of the treasurer are reviewing the financials and taking the lead on the annual budget. Other responsibilities can include: signing promissory notes of the association, signing letters of engagement for reviews or audits of the financials by a third-party public accountant. The treasurer is usually responsible for giving the financial report at the association's annual meeting. The treasurer makes sure that the federal and state tax returns are filed in a timely manner. The treasurer should recommend that a reserve study by an engineering firm be made on a regular basis.

Annual Budget:

The treasurer should take the lead on the association's annual budget. The treasurer does not necessarily compile the actual budget but should work closely with the association manager and supporting accounting staff to ensure the budget is reasonable and ready to present to the entire board of directors for further review and approval. If there is a budget committee formed, the treasurer is usually the chairperson of the committee. At any membership budget ratification meeting, the treasurer will take the lead along with the association president in presenting the budget to the membership.

Annual Meeting Role:

The treasurer's role at the annual meeting is generally limited to a brief financial report. This financial report should be an overview of the financial condition of the association. Typical reports would be the level of funds in operating and reserve accounts as of the year-end. Delinquencies, if they are at a level that affects the operation of the association, can be mentioned in overall amounts, but individual membership delinquencies should not be addressed. If delinquencies are brought up, the treasurer should be prepared to discuss how the delinquencies are being brought to resolution. If the association is taking on additional indebtedness, or issues that could affect the overall financial wellbeing of the association, this should be mentioned during this report.

Outside CPA Firm:

The treasurer should take an active role in the search for and selection of an independent CPA firm to prepare state and federal income tax returns and review or audit the financials. The treasurer is the board's liaison to the association's independent auditor.

174

Delinquencies:

The treasurer is charged with monitoring the collection of delinquent accounts. The treasurer should ensure that the association's management company and attorney are pursuing delinquent accounts efficiently and within the collection guidelines prescribed by the board of directors.

Association Investments:

The treasurer should ensure funds are invested to maximize the yield to the association and invested in approved investment vehicles. The governing documents of the association, many times, will specify how funds are to be invested. They are almost always limited to operating accounts, money market accounts and CDs in federally-insured financial institutions.

D&O Coverage

Directors and Officers (D&O) liability insurance provides coverage in the event of a lawsuit over some board or individual director's act or omission. D&O insurance does not protect the association when a claim is made for personal injury or property damage as a result of negligent actions of the board of directors. Personal injury and property damage claims generally fall under the general liability policy of the association.

However, if a board or individual director knowingly violates the association's governing documents or applicable law, D&O insurance will not generally provide coverage. Each board member is expected to act in good faith and in the best interests of the association. A board member is obligated to apply diligence, obedience, and loyalty in the exercise of their authority. With this authority come these possible grounds for a lawsuit in which D&O coverage may not apply:

- **Conflicts of interest**

- **Mismanagement of funds**

- **Irregular attendance at board meetings**

- **Unwarranted salaries**

- **Misrepresentation**

- **Misstatement of financial condition**

- **Misleading statements**

- **Discretionary practices**

- **Self-dealing**

- **Actions beyond the granted authority**

- **Theft and other criminal activities**

The Great 8

1.Ensure the annual meeting requirements of the governing documents and state statutes have been met. Especially the notification requirements.

2.Meet and shake hands at the door. (see Front Door Solutions)

3.When chairing a meeting do not take questions from the floor until membership open discussion.

4.Leave membership open discussion outside the annual meeting.

5.Staple the "Welcome to the Annual Meeting" form on top of the agenda or the top of the information given out to the membership.

6.Use a "Sign-Up to Speak" sheet for open discussion.

7.Use a lectern for membership open discussion (see The Solid Gold Podium)

8.Stand during the annual meeting. Standing is more authoritative and helps portray confidence.

GLOSSARY OF TERMS

Association Terminology

Certain terms are used incorrectly or generically when discussing association issues. For example, the CC&Rs are often mistakenly referred to as the bylaws, or the membership may believe they are voting for the officers of the board of directors during an annual meeting.

Acclamation or By Acclamation

'By acclamation' is a form of election that does not use a ballot. In the context of a homeowner association annual meeting election, it is most commonly used when there are more available board positions open than candidates running. For example, there are three positions on the board open for election and only one person running. The one person running is elected by acclamation since there is no need to use ballots.

Annual Meeting

A homeowner association annual meeting is a meeting of the membership of the homeowner association. This meeting is required to be held each year for the transaction of association business. Board elections are typically one of these business actions. For business to be conducted and votes to be taken, the membership must have properly received notice of the time, place and date of the meeting within a certain time period, and there must be enough members present to meet the quorum requirement.

Articles of Incorporation

Articles of incorporation are the fundamental charter of an association, which specifies the name, primary purpose, incorporators and any other characteristics, such as being nonprofit. The secretary of state maintains these records in each state.

Assembly

An assembly is used to refer to any group gathered for a common purpose. An annual meeting would be an assembly.

Association Manager

An association manager is a manager of a condominium or homeowner associations. Although traditionally referred to as a property manager, in recent years the profession's title has evolved into association manager.

Bylaws

Bylaws are the written governance of an association. The bylaws are often confused with the articles of incorporation, which only state the basic outline of the company origination. Bylaws generally provide for meetings, elections of a board of directors and officers, filling board vacancies, meeting notices, types and duties of officers, committees, assessments and other routine conduct. To sum up the bylaws, they tell how the association is to be governed. Bylaws are also referred to as the "Rules" of the association.

Chair and Meeting Chair

The chairperson for a meeting is the person who is responsible for presiding over that meeting. The chair is charged with ensuring the meeting is held in accordance with the governing documents of the association and any state statutes. The term Chair, Meeting Chair, Chairperson, Chairman, Chairwoman, Presiding Officer, are all used interchangeably for the person with the responsibility of presiding over a meeting.

Community Association, Common-interest Communities (CIC), or Common-interest Developments (CIDs)

Community Associations include condominiums, townhomes, re-tirement communities, timeshares, and other housing communities made up of individually-owned homes, in addition to shared facilities and common areas.

Condominium Unit

A condominium is a structure, residential or commercial, where own-ership generally involves no direct ownership of land, and ownership is established within vertical and horizontal planes of the structure itself. The condominium owner also has an ownership interest in the common elements. Condominiums, while many times configured in a multi-stack "apartment" type structure, can come in different configurations, such as patio homes or even mobile homes. Condominiums make up approximately 40% of all associations within the United States.

Cooperative Units

Commonly referred to as co-ops, these are structures where ownership is through a corporation, and an owner is a shareholder. Cooperatives can be residential or commercial, and this form of association comprises approximately 5% of the associations within the United States.

Covenants, Conditions and Restrictions (CC&Rs), Declarations, Master Deed or just Covenants

CC&Rs are written and filed with the county register of deeds. They set forth the requirements, limitations, and restrictions on use, as put in place by the developer of an association. CC&Rs may limit size and placement of homes, exterior colors, pets, ages of residents, use of barbecues and other conduct, in order to protect the quiet enjoyment of the various members of the association. CC&Rs are typically enforced by the homeowner association's internal enforcement process that is provided for in the CC&Rs or state statute. These documents are permanent or "run with the land," so future owners are bound to the same requirements.

Declarant

The declarant is usually the developer of the association and can be the home builder of the association. Generally, the declarant who purchases the tract of land either constructs the primary association structure as with a condominium or divides up the tract and sells to builders. Generally, the declarant will build the roads and common elements of the association.

Deliberative Assembly

A Deliberative assembly is a gathering of members, such as members of a homeowner association, who use parliamentary procedure to make decisions.

Director

A director is a member of a board of directors within an association. The membership typically elect directors at an annual meeting. In most cases, a director may also be an officer on the board of directors. However, a director may not necessarily have to be an officer on the board of directors.

Effective Notice

Effective notice is legal notice. With regard to an annual meeting, effective notice is typically when all the association's notice requirements are met per the association's governing documents and placed in the mail or other prescribed delivery methods.

General Consent or Unanimous Consent

In the context of an annual meeting, unanimous consent is a parliamentary procedure in which no member present in the deliberative assembly objects to a proposal. General consent is often used to expedite the consideration of uncontroversial motions. It is, many times, used as a method to reduce procedural steps and thus save time. It can also be referred to as unanimous consent.

Good Standing

A member in good standing is typically regarded as being in compliance of all their explicit obligations of the homeowners' association, while not being subject to any form of sanction, suspension or in litigation with the association. A member not yet adjudicated through a hearing or otherwise not found in violation of the governing documents would typically still be considered in good standing.

Inspectors of Election

Inspectors of election, in the context of a homeowner association annual meeting, is a person or persons appointed to oversee the election process. While tasked with tabulating membership ballots, they determine if votes were properly cast and announce the election results. Interestingly, this title, inspectors of election, is not often used and many times the person or persons charged with overseeing the election process do not know this is their official title.

Officer

An officer is a position on a board of directors: president, vice president, secretary or treasurer. There are instances where other officer titles are found in governing documents, such as chairman, sergeant at arms, assistant secretary and so forth. In even more rare cases, an officer does not necessarily have to be a director. The membership elect directors at an annual meeting, and typically officers are chosen by the directors elected at the annual meeting.

Out of Order

A member is out of order when he or she makes a contemptable motion or action intended to disrupt a meeting and prevent the group from moving forward with the business of the meeting. Motions can be objected to and ruled out of order without debate. In the event the chair does not rule the motion out of order, a two-thirds vote of the group can block further consideration. Behaviors or actions that are not according to the rules of a meeting. Per Roberts Rules of Order, motions that the chair can rule out of order:

- Motions that conflict with the rules, bylaws, or the law.

- Motions that repeat the same question on the same day.

- Motions that conflict with an already adopted motion

- Motions that operate outside the scope or object of the organization

- Motions that appear nonsensical, incorrect, frivolous, or rude

Point of Order

In a formal debate or meeting, a question of whether the correct procedure is being followed.

Quorum

The minimum number of members of an association that must be present at the association's meetings to make the proceedings of that meeting valid.

Parliamentarian

In the United States, a parliamentarian is an expert in the rules and usages of a deliberative assembly or parliamentary procedures.

Rules & Regulations

Rules and regulations are the basic governance of an association. The authority of the association to establish reasonable rules and regulations is generally set forth in the CC&Rs. Rules and regulations usually expand on what is established in the CC&Rs. For example, the CC&R may set forth that the association swimming pool is for the exclusive use of members and their guests, while the rules and regulations may specify that a member is limited to 3 guests at one time.

Special Meeting

A special meeting is a meeting that can typically be called by the association president, board of directors, and possibly the membership. Quorum and notification requirements may be higher or more stringent than the association's annual meeting.

Substitute Annual Meeting

A substitute annual meeting provision in an association's governing documents allows for another date and time to be designated for the annual meeting that is different than what is prescribed by the bylaws. A meeting called under this provision shall be designated and treated for all, intents and purposes as the annual meeting.

Suspend the Rules

In the context of an annual meeting, suspension of the rules allows the assembly to set aside its normal rules to do something that it could not do otherwise - such as moving agenda items around to accommodate another agenda item.

Townhome

A townhome is a structure usually attached to other similar like structures, where the ownership of the structure includes the land beneath. It is typically configured with two or more levels.

Unanimous Consent or General Consent

In the context of an annual meeting, unanimous consent is a parliamentary procedure in which no member present in the deliberative assembly objects to a proposal. Unanimous consent is often used to expedite the consideration of uncontroversial motions. It is, many times, used as a method to reduce procedural steps and thus save time. It can also be referred to as general consent.

APPENDIX

Robert's Rules of Orders – A Brief Overview

Robert's Rules of Order is the book on parliamentary procedure that is considered the standard. It is recognized as the standard by many statutes and organizations. Parliamentarians, associations, clubs, groups or any organization with a deliberative body generally recognize this book as the authoritative guide to conducting an orderly and equitable meeting.

Brigadier General, Henry M. Robert, graduated from the United States Military Academy in 1857 and received a commission in the Army. He was once asked to chair a church meeting and became embarrassed because of his lack of knowledge regarding parliamentary procedure. This embarrassment left him determined to understand parliamentary procedure better. During his military service, he was posted to different parts of the United States, where he found varying forms of parliamentary procedure being followed. In 1876, he decided to publish a standardized manual, and this manual eventually became *Robert's Rules of Order*.

Robert's Rules of Order, Newly Revised, is an excellent resource for a board of directors. It is advisable to have a copy at all membership meetings. While *Robert's Rules of Order* has a great deal of reference material within the covers, gaining an overall working grasp of parliamentary procedures is obtainable without memorizing every section of the book.

Five Key Aspects of Robert's Rules of Order:

1. The meeting Chair decides who has the floor.

2. Only one person may have the floor or speak at a time.

3. The person with the floor may only discuss the issue being considered.

4. Individuals cannot speak a second time if someone who hasn't spoken for the first time wants the floor to speak.

5. It is the responsibility of the Chair to move the meeting along in a timely fashion.

Membership Survey

1) Since you have purchased your home, would you say the community has:

- Improved

- Somewhat Improved

- About the Same

- Somewhat Worsened

- Worsened

2) Complete this statement: "I enjoy living in the Happy Glen Community because..."

Check all that apply

- Assessment

- Neighbors/Friends

- Amenities

- Board of Directors

- Location of Community

- Association/Property Manager

- Other _____

3) Complete this statement: "Things I do not like about living in the Happy Glen Community..."

Check all that apply

- Assessment

- Neighbors/Friends

- Amenities

- Board of Directors

- Location of Community

- Association/Property Manager

- Other _____

4) Complete this statement: "The board of directors is doing a(n)..."

- Great Job

- Above Average Job

- Ok Job

- Below Average Job

- Terrible Job

5) Complete this statement: "The association/property manager is doing a(n)..."

- Great Job

- Above Average Job

- Ok Job

- Below Average Job

- Terrible Job

6) What would improve the association the most in your opinion:

_____

_____

_____

_____

_____

Seating Configuration

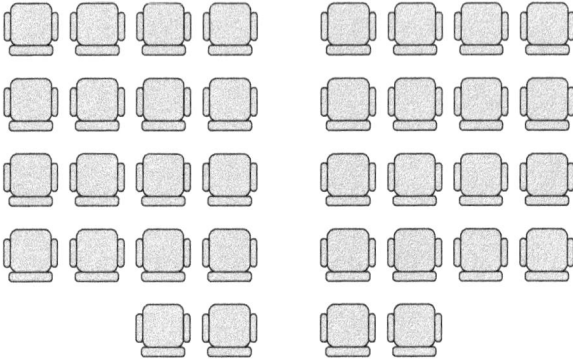

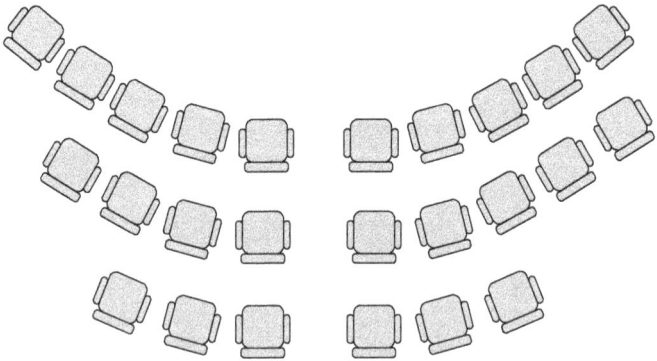

VOTING CERTIFICATE

A Voting Certificate is used to determine who the voting representative will be if there are multiple owners, corporate owners, trust, or other entity of a home in our community. Please note the following:

1) "Voting Certificate" means a document which designates one of the recorded title owners, or a corporate, partnership, or entity representative, who is authorized to vote on that behalf of the entity.

2) If a corporation, partnership, joint venture or other entity is the fee simple title holder to a home, or more than one person owns the home, the homeowner shall designate one person as the Member entitled to cast votes and/or to approve or disapprove matters as may be required or provided by these Articles, the Bylaws or the Declaration(s) of Condominium(s).

CERTIFICATE OF APPOINTMENT OF VOTING REPRESENTATIVE

To the Secretary of Happy Glen Homeowner Association, Inc. (the "Association") THIS IS TO CERTIFY that the undersigned, constituting all of the record owner(s) of _____ Address in Happy Glen HOA _____, A single family home, have designated _____
_____
(Name of Voting Representative) as the representative to cast all votes and to express all approvals that such owners may be entitled to cast or express at all meetings of the membership of the Association and for all other purposes provided by the Declaration, the Articles and Bylaws of the Association.

The following examples illustrate the proper use of this Certificate:

(i) Unit owned by only one person: No Voting Certificate required.

(ii) Unit owned by more than one person (including husband and wife), A Voting Certificate is required and must be signed by ALL owners.

(iii) Unit owned by ABC, Inc., a corporation. Voting Certificate must be filed with the board secretary designating an officer or employee entitled to vote, signed by an officer of the entity, and attested to by the secretary of the entity.

(iv) Unit owned in the name of a Trust; the current trustee must sign the Voting Certificate.

This Certificate is made pursuant to the Articles of Incorporation and shall revoke all prior Certificates and be valid until revoked by a subsequent Voting Certificate.

DATED: _____ _____, 20_____.

Owner:

Owner:

Owner:

If Corporation or other entity:

Title:

If corporation Attested by:

Preliminary Steps Check Sheet

Association Name: _____

Annual Meeting Preliminary Steps:

   Annual Meeting Date: _____ / _____ / _____

   Annual Meeting Start Time: _____

   Annual Meeting Location & Address: _____

_____

   Location Closing Time or Time Meeting Must Be Over: _____

   Location Reservation Contact: _____

   Location Reservation Contact Phone #: _____

   Location Fee: $_____

   Location Fee Check Cut Date: _____

Written Notification Time Requirements:

   No More Than _____ days before annual meeting

   No Less Than _____ days before annual meeting

   Notification Mailing Date: _____ / _____ / _____

Notification Mailing Items:

   Notice of Annual Meeting _____

   Nominating Application _____

   Proxy _____

Double check association documents to make sure no other items are required to be mailed out with annual meeting notification mailing. For example: HOA Annual Budget, Agenda, etc.

Date Notification Items Mailed: _____ / _____ / _____

Affidavit of Mailing Completed

Annual Meeting Check Sheet:
Items to take or note

Association Name: _____

___Owner List Alphabetical Order with Signature Line

(Highlight names in yellow to make sign-in faster)

___Owner List by Address to verify against Alphabetical List

___Returned Nominating Applications

___Returned Proxies

___Quorum Requirement: _____ % of Membership

___Quorum Requirement: _____ Actual Number in Person or by Proxy

___Percentage Ownership Spreadsheet to Calculate Quorum & ___ Votes (If Applicable)

___Agenda * (Staple & make a packet of all handouts) Put Welcome to The Annual Meeting Sheet on top of the Agenda

___Last Annual Meeting Minutes *

___Ballots * (Check Documents to see if everyone gets one vote or if it's by percentage ownership)

___Association's Documents, CC&Rs, Bylaws and Rules & Regs.

    ___Last 12/31 Income Statement **

    ___Current Budget **

    ___Last Complete Month's Balance Sheet

    ___*Robert's Rules of Order*

    ___Notice of Annual Meeting with Affidavit of Mailing

    ___Recent Audit Report

    ___Blank Proxies and Blank Nominating Application ***

    ___Delinquency Owner List ****

___Double check association documents to make sure no other items are required to be provided to membership during Annual Meeting. For example, a copy of last year's audit.

* Copies an estimate of total attendance plus 20% more

** Copies determined by what board wants to distribute

*** Five copies for members who come and must leave

**** If governing documents and board of directors require this for voting

Example of an Affidavit of Mailing

AFFIDAVIT OF MAILING

I, _____, of lawful age upon his oath deposes and says: that he mailed to all _____ _____ property owners of record as of _____ _____, a letter containing information regarding the Annual Meeting of said Association to be held on this application on _____
. A copy of the typical letter and names and addresses of all _____ _____ property owners of record are attached and made a part of this Affidavit.

That said mailing was made on _____

_____

Signature

STATE OF NORTH CAROLINA   COUNTY OF _____)

The above and foregoing Affidavit as subscribed before me on this _____ day of _____, _____, A.D. personally by _____ _____.

_____

Notary Public

My Commission Expires: _____

Percentage Ownership Ballot Calculation Matrix

	John Smith	Berry Jones	Lisa Smith	Kelly Jones	Nancy Smith
0.028					
0.03					
0.038					
0.044					
0.049					

HAPPY GLEN HOA
HOMEOWNER CONCERNS FORM

The Board of Directors is requesting that all homeowners list any issues or concerns that they may have regarding the community in the space below. The Board will review everything submitted and respond in the coming weeks. Thank you for taking the time to share your concerns.

_____
_____
_____
_____
_____
_____
_____
_____
_____
_____
_____
_____
_____
_____
_____
_____
_____

HOMEOWNER NAME: _____
_____

HOMEOWNER ADDRESS: _____
_____

CONTACT PHONE NUMBER: _____
_____

CONTACT EMAIL ADDRESS: _____
_____

INDEX

C

D

E

F

G

H

I

L

M

N

O

R

S

W

ABOUT THE AUTHOR:

Since 2003 Chris has been the president of William Douglas Management, Inc., an association management company with offices in North Carolina, South Carolina, and Georgia. He received a BA in Business Management from North Carolina States University. Chris resides with his family in North Carolina.

www.ingramcontent.com/pod-product-compliance
Lightning Source LLC
Chambersburg PA
CBHW031358180326
41458CB00043B/6537/J